Michael Price

Windows 10 for Seniors

3rd edition

for PCs, Laptops and Touch devices

In easy steps is an imprint of In Easy Steps Limited
16 Hamilton Terrace · Holly Walk · Leamington Spa
Warwickshire · United Kingdom · CV32 4LY
www.ineasysteps.com

Third Edition

Notice of Liability
Every effort has been made to ensure that this book
contains accurate and current information. However, In
Easy Steps Limited and the author shall not be liable for
any loss or damage suffered by readers as a result of
any information contained herein.

Trademarks
Microsoft® and Windows® are registered trademarks
of Microsoft Corporation. All other trademarks
are acknowledged as belonging to their respective
companies.

In Easy Steps Limited supports The Forest Stewardship
Council (FSC), the leading international forest
certification organization. All our titles that are printed
on Greenpeace approved FSC certified paper carry the
FSC logo.

MIX
Paper from
responsible sources
FSC® C020837

Printed and bound in the United Kingdom

ISBN 978-1-84078-811-2

Contents

12 Networking   207

13 Security & Maintenance   219

Index   233

1 Get Windows 10

This chapter explains how Windows 10 has evolved, identifies the new features, and helps you recognize what's needed to upgrade your existing computer. You can upgrade to the appropriate edition of Windows 10, and sign in to its redesigned Start menu Desktop or work in the new Tablet mode.

Windows 10

Windows 10 is the latest release of Microsoft Windows, the operating system for personal computers. There has been a long list of Windows releases, including:

- 1995   Windows 95
- 1998   Windows 98
- 2000   Windows Me
- 2001   Windows XP
- 2003   Windows XP MCE
- 2007   Windows Vista
- 2009   Windows 7
- 2012   Windows 8 and Windows RT
- 2013   Windows 8.1 and Windows 8.1 RT
- 2014   Windows 8.1 and 8.1 RT Update 1
- 2015   Windows 10 and its updates

When you buy a new computer, it is usually shipped with the latest available release of Windows. This takes advantage of the hardware features generally available at the time. Each year sees new and more powerful features being incorporated into the latest computers. In line with this, the requirements for Microsoft Windows have increased steadily. For example, the minimum and recommended amounts of system memory have increased from 4MB to 8MB in Windows 95, and 1GB to 2GB in Windows 10. There's a similar progression in terms of the processor power, the video graphics facilities and hard disk storage.

This means that your computer may need upgrading or extending in order to use a later release of Windows, especially if you want to take advantage of new capabilities such as Multitouch. To take full advantage of new features you may need a new computer; for example, a tablet PC.

Each release enhances existing features and adds new facilities. Thus, the new Windows 10 is able to support all the functions of Windows 8.1, Windows 8, Windows 7 and prior releases, often with enhancements, plus its own unique new features. This allows you to use your computer to carry out tasks that might not have been supported with previous releases of the operating system.

Don't forget

Within each Microsoft Windows release there are several editions catering for different types of users, such as Home, Pro and Enterprise (see page 16).

Hot tip

Windows RT and 8.1 RT are versions of Windows designed for tablet PCs with the ARM processor, used in cell phones, etc. These devices are now supported by Windows 10 Mobile.

Hot tip

From Windows 7 onwards, the requirements are more standardized, so there's less need for changes to processor, memory or storage specifications.

Which Release is Installed?

To check which release of Windows is currently installed on your system, you can look at the System panel.

1 Press the WinKey + Pause key in any version of Windows to display the System panel

2 The operating system details will be shown (along with user, memory and processor information)

WinKey is normally used to represent the Windows Logo key. The Pause key is normally labeled Pause/Break.

These images show the System panel for computers with:

Windows 7

Windows 8.1 Pro

Windows RT 8.1

Windows 10 Pro

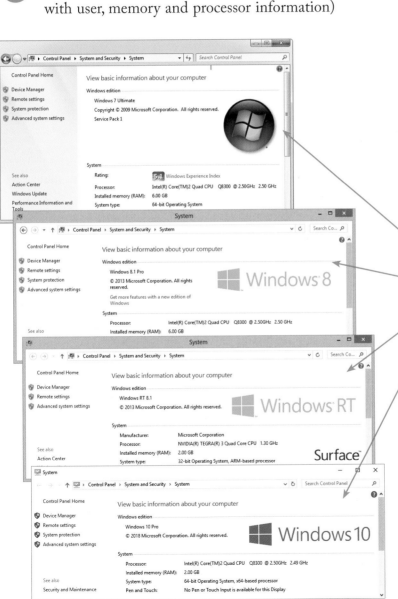

The System panel shows the Windows edition and service level. Other details vary; e.g. versions after Windows 7 have no Experience Index (system rating).

Versions of Windows

You can check which updates have been applied to your copy of Windows, whichever release you have installed on your system.

1 Press WinKey + R to initiate the Run command box

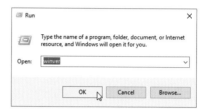

2 Type winver and click OK

3 Click OK to close the Windows Version panel

For Windows 10, there are numerous versions you might see, since there is a major update every six months or so.

The versions currently available include:

Version	Name	Date Released
● 1507	Original Release	Jul 2015
● 1511	November Update	Nov 2015
● 1607	Anniversary Update	Aug 2016
● 1703	Creators Update	Apr 2017
● 1709	Fall Creators Update	Oct 2017
● 1803	April 2018 Update	Apr 2018
● 1809	To be announced	Oct 2018

Features of Windows 10

Windows 10 retains the tablet PC and touch capabilities that were introduced in Windows 8, while reintroducing the familiar Start menu and Desktop from earlier versions, along with an improved, more secure operating system with a new browser, the Cortana Personal Digital Assistant, Office functionality and other ease of use facilities. Windows 10 is also designed to run on Windows phones, small tablets, and other devices such as the Xbox One.

It was free to upgrade during the first year, for systems with Windows 7 or Windows 8.1, or for Windows Phone 8.1 users. Upgrades now cost $119.99/£119.99 upwards.

Universal Apps

What used to be called Modern apps or Microsoft Store apps are now known as Universal apps, because the same code can be used to run on a variety of devices, not just PCs.

There's a new Microsoft Store for Windows 10, where you can download desktop programs as well as the Universal apps. These include Office for Windows apps such as Word, Excel, Outlook Mail and Calendar.

Start Menu

Windows 10 replaces the Windows 8 Start screen with a Start menu that provides a scrollable list of programs (frequently used and recently installed, or all programs) in a single column, with the rest of the pane assigned to app tiles. You can resize this pane or make it full-screen.

Task Switcher with Timeline

To display all running apps and programs, there's a task switcher with large thumbnails that appears when you press Alt + Tab, or when you select Task View from the Taskbar. It includes Timeline, which gives access to your history of activities, including those on other PCs you've signed on to.

Snap Assist

Since Universal apps now run in windows on the Desktop, just like programs, Split Screen View has been replaced by

The Start menu returns in place of the Start screen introduced in Windows 8, and the Desktop is used for Universal apps as well as traditional Windows applications.

There are some new Windows 10 apps and some traditional desktop applications (now commonly known as Windows Classic apps) provided with Windows 10 at installation, but you may need to visit the Microsoft Store for some functions that were previously included.

...cont'd

Snap View, where you can drag windows into the corners of the screen. You can use all four corners and have each window take up a quarter of the screen, to have up to four programs or apps displayed.

Multiple Desktops

When you have a number of windows active, and you don't have multiple monitors, you can put the windows on multiple virtual Desktops, to manage several projects or to separate personal and business activities.

Tablet Mode

As an alternative for touch-enabled systems, you can change the appearance of Windows 10 by turning on Tablet mode, either via the appropriate setting or by removing or folding the keyboard on a hybrid or convertible PC.

The Taskbar is removed, and you have a full-screen Start menu that shows the tiles and hides the scrolling list of apps. All your windows switch to full-screen, or you can use Snap View with two apps displayed simultaneously.

File Explorer

File Explorer is a file management app in Windows. The Navigation bar in File Explorer now includes the new Home command and a Quick Access list of frequently visited locations and folders, plus a list of recently opened files underneath it.

Microsoft Edge Browser

Microsoft has replaced the aging Internet Explorer with the new Edge browser, with better support for web standards and faster speed. Internet Explorer is still available in Windows 10 for those websites that aren't compatible with Edge.

Cortana Personal Digital Assistant

This was introduced in the Windows Phone, and appears as a Search box on the Taskbar, with voice access. You can search the Start menu; installed apps; documents; apps from the Store; and search results from the web. Cortana also lets you speak to your PC to do simple tasks such as set reminders, book appointments, make calculations, and even identify songs!

What's Needed

The minimum configuration recommended by Microsoft to install and run Windows 10 is as follows:

- Processor   1GHz 32-bit or 64-bit.

- System memory   1GB (32-bit) or 2GB (64-bit).

- Graphics   DirectX 9 graphics device with WDDM 1.0 driver.

- Hard disk drive   16GB (32-bit) or 20GB (64-bit) free.

- Optical drive   DVD/CD (for installation purposes).

- Display   SVGA monitor with 1024 x 600 or higher resolution.

There may be additional requirements for some features; for example:

- Internet access for online services and features such as Windows Update.

- Five-point Multitouch hardware for touch functions.

- A network and multiple PCs running Windows 10 for HomeGroup file and printer sharing.

- An optical drive with rewriter function for DVD/CD authoring and backup function.

- Trusted Platform Module (TPM) 1.2 hardware for BitLocker encryption.

- USB flash drive for BitLocker To Go.

- Audio output (headphones or speakers) for music and sound in Windows Media Player.

If you were running Windows 7 or Windows 8.1, your system would have qualified for the Windows 10 upgrade. However, you needed the latest versions of those systems: Windows 7 with Service Pack 1, or Windows 8.1 with Update 1. Windows Update would detect this automatically and add the Get Windows 10 app to the system tray, if your system is eligible.

The terms 32-bit and 64-bit relate to the way the processor handles memory. You'll also see the terms x86 and x64 used for 32-bit and 64-bit respectively.

The product functions and the graphics capabilities may vary depending on the system configuration.

The Home edition has the Microsoft Edge browser, and apps such as Photos, Maps, Mail, Calendar, Music, and Video. It even includes Xbox One integration, to allow you to access your games libraries.

Home and Pro are available as retail packages. Pro is also available under the Volume Licensing program, intended for purchasing in bulk, and is the only way to obtain the Enterprise and Education editions.

The IoT Core edition offers the prospect of remotely managing your home via Windows 10.

Windows 10 Editions

Microsoft provides various editions of Windows 10, to suit various groups of users:

Windows 10 Home
This is for home and personal use, and includes all the essential features for desktops, laptops, tablet PCs and hybrid computers.

Windows 10 Mobile
Evolving from the Windows Phone, Windows 10 Mobile provides apps equivalent to the desktop PC range, including Microsoft Office apps such as Word, Excel, and PowerPoint, for mobile phone and tablet users.

This edition is still supported for existing devices, but is no longer being developed or extended.

Windows 10 Pro
In addition to all the features of Windows 10 Home, this edition adds apps and utilities for small businesses, including Secure Boot, Device Guard, and Cloud technology support. Pro is for PC enthusiasts, professionals and small business users.

Windows 10 Enterprise
Building on Windows 10 Pro, Windows 10 Enterprise adds advanced capabilities to protect devices, identities, applications and sensitive information. This edition is for medium and large organizations.

Windows 10 Education
Microsoft provides a version of Windows 10 explicitly for academic purposes. Similar in content to Windows 10 Enterprise, this is for schools, universities and students.

Windows 10 IoT Core
Finally, Windows 10 IoT Core will run customizable versions of Windows 10 on household appliances like smart thermostats, factory machinery, and even toasters.

Selecting Your Edition

Your choice of Windows 10 edition may be predetermined by the type of equipment you are using, or by the organization you belong to.

However, if you are an individual user or a member of a small business, and you are using a desktop computer, laptop, tablet PC or hybrid PC, then you may need to look more closely at the particular options in the Home, Pro, Education and Enterprise editions. Some of the features to look at are:

Features	Home	Pro	Enterprise	Education
Customizable Start menu	Y	Y	Y	Y
Windows Defender & Windows Firewall	Y	Y	Y	Y
Fast start with Hiberboot & InstantGo	Y	Y	Y	Y
TPM support	Y	Y	Y	Y
Battery Saver	Y	Y	Y	Y
Windows Update	Y	Y	Y	Y
Cortana Personal Digital Assistant	Y	Y	Y	Y
Windows Hello login	Y	Y	Y	Y
Virtual desktops	Y	Y	Y	Y
Snap Assist	Y	Y	Y	Y
Continuum Tablet & Desktop modes	Y	Y	Y	Y
Microsoft Edge	Y	Y	Y	Y
Device Encryption	Y	Y	Y	Y
Easy Upgrade Home to Education	Y	-	-	Y
Easy Upgrade Pro to Enterprise	-	Y	Y	-
Group Policy Management	-	Y	Y	Y
BitLocker	-	Y	Y	Y
Remote Desktop	-	Y	Y	Y
Windows Update for Business	-	Y	Y	Y
Direct Access	-	Y	Y	Y
Windows To Go Creator	-	-	Y	Y
Start Screen Control with Group Policy	-	-	Y	Y
AppLocker	-	-	Y	Y
BranchCache	-	-	Y	Y

18

Upgrade to Windows 10

If you are planning to install Windows 10 on an existing computer running a previous version of Windows, you may be able to upgrade and retain your existing Windows settings, personal data and applications.

The upgrade paths available include:

● Upgrade to the Windows 10 Home edition from Windows 7 Starter, Windows 7 Home Basic or Windows 7 Home Premium editions.

● Upgrade to the Windows 10 Pro edition from Windows 7 Professional and Windows Ultimate editions.

● Upgrade to the Windows 10 Home edition from Windows 8.1 base edition.

● Upgrade to the Windows 10 Pro edition from Windows 8.1 Pro edition.

● Upgrade to the Windows 10 Enterprise edition from Windows 7 Enterprise edition.

● Upgrade to the Windows 10 Enterprise edition from Windows 8/8.1 Enterprise editions.

You won't be able to upgrade or retain Windows settings, personal data and applications if you make a move between 32-bit and 64-bit configurations, whichever edition of Windows you are using.

There is no upgrade path to Windows 10 offered for Windows 8.1 RT for the Microsoft Surface RT and similar devices. However, the Windows 8.1 RT Update 3, delivered in September 2015 via the Windows Update service, added some Windows 10 functionality. For example, it gave Windows 8.1 RT the capability of using a Start menu similar to that in Windows 10, in place of the Start screen. This is implemented as an option managed via Taskbar Properties.

Prepare to Install

When you received
notification that your
upgrade was ready, you
could upgrade your existing
Windows to Windows 10, via
Windows Update.

You may also install Windows 10
from a DVD, running the Setup
program included on this.

In either case, you can
retain the Windows
settings, personal files
and apps from your
existing system (see
page 20).

1 Follow the prompts to
install Windows 10

2 Allow current updates to be added during the install

3 You'll be told of any issues or concerns that may
apply to your system

If you choose not to
apply current updates
at this time, they can
be added later via
Windows Update.

In this example, there's a change of display language.
However, this can be adjusted later if required, after the
installation has completed.

Installing Windows 10

1 Choose to retain your existing Windows settings, personal files and apps, and click Install

2 You are warned that your PC will restart several times as the installation proceeds

3 A progress report will be displayed as files are copied, features and drivers are installed, and settings are configured

4 If you are upgrading from Windows 8.1, your existing Microsoft Account will be detected

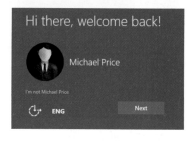

You can switch to a different Microsoft Account if you wish. With upgrades from Windows 7, you'll be asked to provide an existing Microsoft Account or create a new one.

20

...cont'd

5 As the installation continues, you'll get information updates such as details of the new apps available

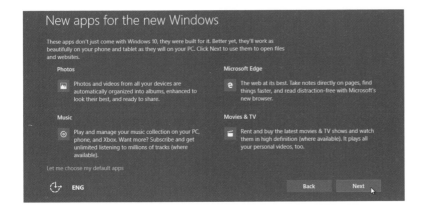

6 When the installation completes, you'll see the Lock screen, from where you can sign in to your account

7 Click or swipe up to enter your account details (see page 28) and start a session

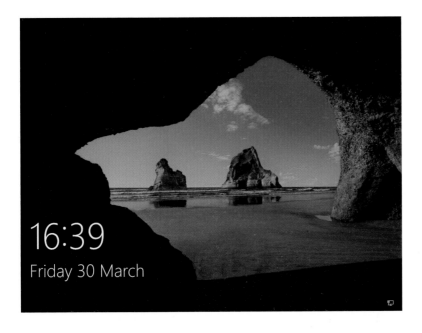

Windows 10 has new versions of the Photos and Music apps, plus the Microsoft Edge browser that replaces Internet Explorer. There is also an app for Movies and TV. All these apps will run on your smartphone and your tablet as well as on your PC.

You can change the image that is displayed on the Lock screen, and even provide your own image (see page 63 for details).

Create a Fresh System

You can install Windows 10 from a DVD to create a fresh new system on a new PC, or to completely replace the existing system on your current computer:

When Windows 10 is installed from a DVD onto an existing system, you will lose the current data files and settings.

1 Setup proceeds to copy files, and then installs features and updates

2 You may be asked to provide the product key required to activate your copy of Windows 10

You need to identify company PCs as such, so that they can be set up to access the resources of your organization.

3 Identify your PC as a personal system, or a company machine provided to you for business purposes

4 Provide your Microsoft Account email address and password, or choose to create a new account

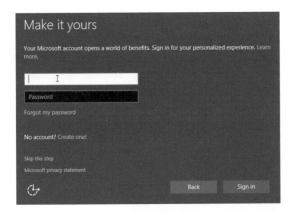

You can skip this step, and start off with a Local Account that won't have access to the Microsoft Store.

5 You can set up a four-digit PIN code to use as an alternative to your account password

A Personal Identification Number (PIN) code is faster to use, yet even more secure than your password.

6 If you are connected to your home or work network, you should choose to make the PC discoverable by other PCs on the network

Do not allow your PC to be discoverable if you are setting it up on a public network such as at a library or airport location.

Your Windows Apps

When you start Windows 10, you can see the apps and programs that are provided. These vary depending on the type of Windows 10 installation.

1 From the Lock screen, sign in using your PIN code or password (see pages 28-30) to display the Desktop

2 On the Desktop, click the Start button at the left of the Taskbar (or press or tap the WinKey)

3 The Windows 10 Start menu displays Recently added, Most used and the All Apps list, plus a panel of app tiles, like the Windows 8/8.1 Start screen

24

4 Scroll the All Apps list to see the apps and programs

Entries with a Folder icon expand when you click them and contain groups of items, for example:

5 On a tablet PC, or hybrid PC without a keyboard, the Start menu displays in full-screen Tablet mode

In Tablet mode, click the All apps button to show three columns of Recently added, Most used and All apps.

Click the Pinned tiles button to restore the full-screen Start menu.

Closing Windows 10

When you finish working with Windows 10, you'll want to Shut down or Sign out. Here are three examples:

1 As with Windows 8.1, you can right-click the Start button and select Shut down or sign out, then choose the required option

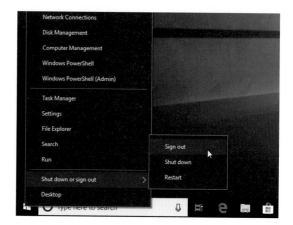

Sign out	Sleep
Sleep	Shut down
Shut down	Restart
Restart	

You can use Sleep when you're going to be away from your PC for a while. It uses very little power, and when you return and touch the screen or move the mouse, the PC starts up quickly, and you're back to where you left off.

2 On the Start menu, click the Power button to select Shut down or Restart

3 The Power button menu is also available in Tablet mode

2 Windows 10 Interface

Windows 10 uses the tile-based interface first seen in Windows 8. It is designed for touch operation, while still supporting keyboard and mouse, and features a new form of Start menu and new ways to arrange and manage windows.

Hot tip

The start-up time depends on the configuration of your computer and how it was previously closed down, but usually it is less than a minute.

Hot tip

This is one of the supplied Lock screen images, but you can choose another image from the Pictures library (see pages 63 and 96), or even play a slideshow.

Start Windows 10

Switch on your computer to start up the operating system. The stages are as follows:

1 A simple Windows logo is displayed, with a rotating cursor to show that the system is being loaded

2 After a while, the Lock screen is displayed

18:04
Friday 30 March

3 Press any key, click a mouse button, or swipe up on a touchscreen monitor to display the user Sign-in screen

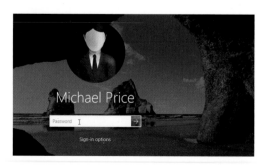

Michael Price

Password

Sign-in options

...cont'd

4 Type the password and click the arrow (or press the Enter key)

If there are multiple user accounts, you may need to select the required account before signing in (see page 31).

5 The Welcome message is displayed while the user account settings are being applied

An error message is displayed if you mistype the password.

29

6 The Windows 10 Desktop screen is displayed, showing the image associated with your account

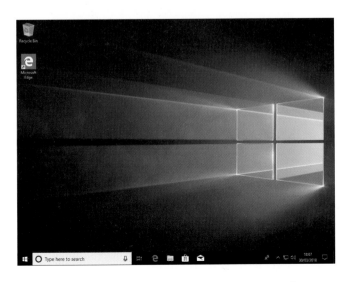

If you have Tablet mode enabled on your system, it may go straight to the Start menu display (see page 25).

Sign-in options may also include the Picture password option (see pages 74-75) if you have defined one for your account.

Windows remembers the last Sign-in option used, and presents that option the next time you sign in to that account.

PIN Code Sign-in

If you specified a PIN code during install (see page 23), or added one later using Settings (see page 76) you can sign in using this.

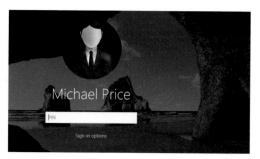

1 The Sign-in screen will request the PIN code

2 To revert to the Password, select Sign-in options and click the Password button

3 To sign in with the PIN code, just type the four digits – there is no arrow to click and no need to press Enter

4 The Desktop (or Start menu if Tablet mode is enabled) will be displayed

Multiple User Accounts

1 If you want a different account from the one selected, click the required account in the list

If there is more than one user account, the Sign-in screen will display the last used account, along with the list of available accounts. (See pages 86-87 for how to add other users.)

2 Enter the password to sign in to the selected account

31

3 The Welcome message is displayed while the account details are being loaded

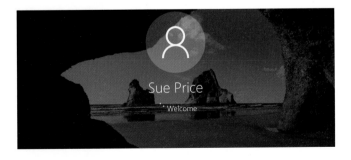

Where there's no email address shown for an account in the list, you'll know it is a Local Account rather than a Microsoft Account, and so cannot be used to download content from the Microsoft Store.

4 The Desktop screen or the Tablet mode panel will be displayed, as appropriate for the selected device

Desktop Layout

The standard PC with mouse and keyboard, without Tablet mode enabled, starts with the Desktop screen. This is similar to the display from earlier versions of Windows, with Desktop icons, and the Taskbar with Start button, Shortcuts, and Taskbar icons. This example shows both Classic apps and Universal apps running in windows on the Desktop.

Hot tip

Click in the Search box on the Taskbar to get started with Cortana, and click the Settings icon (see the illustration on page 33) to review the options.

Desktop Icon   Universal App   Classic App   Background

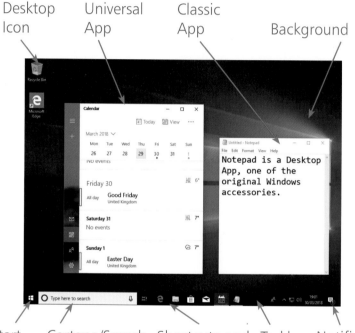

Notepad is a Desktop App, one of the original Windows accessories.

Start Button   Cortana/Search Box   Shortcuts and Active Apps   Taskbar   Notification Area

Hot tip

In previous versions of Windows, the Notification area was known as the System Tray. The Action Center displayed from here includes features that were on the Windows 8/8.1 Charms bar.

Click the Action Center icon to the right of date/time in the Notification area, to display the Action Center. This is a full-height bar on the right of the screen. It contains a set of Quick Actions for toggling functions on or off. You can enable Tablet mode for example, or Connect to a network. There's also a shortcut to Settings. Above these Quick Actions, details of any Notifications will be displayed.

Click the Start button to display the Start menu; a merger of the features of the Start menu and the Start screen from previous versions of Windows.

Most Used   Recently Added   App Group   Live Tile

Settings, Power etc.   All Apps   Shortcuts and Active Apps   Action Center Button

1. Scroll the All Apps list (see page 37) to see the full set of apps on your system (see page 25)

2. The full Taskbar is shown with the Start menu. It includes the Start button, the Search box, shortcuts, active apps and the Notification area

3. Right-click the File Explorer icon to get quick access to parts of the file system, such as Documents, Pictures, Downloads and the Desktop

Hot tip

You can click and drag the edges of the Start menu panel to change the size of the panel and the number of tiles displayed.

Don't forget

To close the Start menu and redisplay the Desktop, click the Start button (or press WinKey).

33

Don't forget

Click the Expand button to add titles to the column of icons on the left-hand side of the Start screen.

Tablet Mode Layout

A tablet PC, or a hybrid PC with the keyboard removed or folded, will start up in Tablet mode with the full-screen version of the Start menu.

Hot tip

Windows 10 includes Continuum technology, which allows your system to transition between states manually or automatically; e.g. from using a keyboard, to touchscreen when you remove or fold the keyboard on a hybrid PC.

Display Most Used and Recently Added   App Group   Live Tile

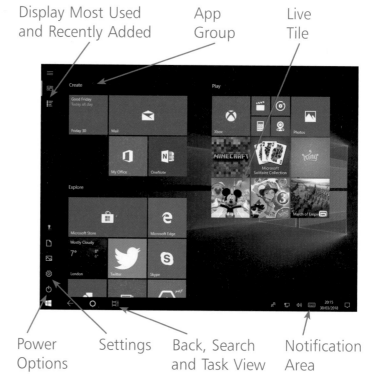

Power Options   Settings   Back, Search and Task View   Notification Area

The Taskbar is abbreviated, with just the Start, Back, Search and Task View buttons plus the Notification area, but no shortcuts or active apps. You can enable the full Taskbar via Settings, if you wish.

Don't forget

If you have multiple monitors defined on your PC, then Tablet mode is disabled and cannot be activated until you revert to a single monitor.

1   Click the Action Center icon to display the Action Center with Quick Actions and Notifications

You can enable and disable Tablet mode on any PC, using the Tablet mode toggle displayed on the Action Center, or via Settings, as described on page 35.

...cont'd

To enable, configure or disable Tablet mode from Settings:

1 Select Settings from the Start menu, or All settings from the Action Center

2 Select the System option from Settings

These options to invoke Settings are available whether or not Tablet mode is already enabled.

3 Select the Tablet mode entry and review the settings

When Tablet mode is turned on, all apps (Classic and Universal apps) will run full-screen.

- Specify the action to be taken when you sign in

- Control how automatic switching takes place

- Hide or show app icons on the Taskbar

- You can also choose to hide or show the Taskbar itself

35

Power User Menu

There's a menu of useful shortcuts associated with the Start button (at the left of the Cortana/Search box).

1 Right-click the Start button to display the menu

2 Alternatively, press WinKey + X to display that same menu

This allows you to access a set of functions that is often needed by the more advanced user, which includes the System panel, Device Manager, Disk Management, Windows PowerShell, Task Manager, Settings, and Run.

Select the Shut down or sign out option, and you can choose to Sign out, Shut down or Restart your system.

Make sure that it's the Start button that you right-click, or you'll get the right-click action associated with the alternative area you click. On the Desktop, for example, you would get the Screen menu with View, Sort by, etc.

On the Taskbar, you'd get a menu with related options including Toolbars, Task Manager and Taskbar settings. This opens Settings at Personalization, with Taskbar selected, so you can adjust the Taskbar Properties.

Moving Around

You can explore the contents of the Start menu in the right-hand tiled area to see which of the apps on your system have been pinned to the Start menu. If there are some apps off-screen, use the scroll bar that appears at the right of the panel when you move the mouse. The tiled area also slides vertically when the mouse is hovering over this area and you roll the mouse wheel up or down.

Hot tip

With a Multitouch monitor or tablet PC in Desktop or Tablet mode, you simply drag the screen up or down as necessary to display other tiles and groups of tiles.

Scroll Bar

There's also a scroll bar displayed when you move the mouse over the tiled area of the Start menu in Tablet mode. You can also slide the area vertically with the mouse wheel, if you have a mouse connected to your tablet PC.

Don't forget

With a desktop PC in Tablet mode, you can also use the four keyboard arrows to navigate through the app tiles to locate the one you want.

Scroll Bar

Start an App

Universal apps can be represented on the Start menu by Static tiles, or by Live tiles that display dynamic information from the associated apps, even when they are not running.

1 To start an app, move the mouse pointer over the tile for the desired app and left-click to load it

2 This example uses Tablet mode, so the app loads full-screen, with weather details for the default location

3 Switch back to the Start menu and choose another Universal app; for example, select Money

4 In Tablet mode, this app would open full-screen, overlaying the previous app

In the example on the following page, Tablet mode has been disabled, so the selected app opens as a window on the Desktop rather than full-screen.

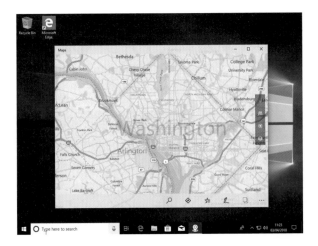

When you have several apps running, you can show all the active apps and choose the one to work with next.

1 Click the Task View button (or press WinKey + Tab) to show all the apps, and click on the required app

When you have several active apps, the Snap Assist option will allow you to display up to four apps on the screen (see pages 40-41).

Task View includes Timeline, which shows the history of activities on this PC and on other PCs where you sign on with the same Microsoft ID.

2 Alternatively, hold down Alt and tap the Tab key until the app you want is selected, then release Alt

Snap Apps

Universal apps and Classic apps can be arranged using the Snap Assist feature. You can display up to four apps.

1 Open several apps as windows on the Desktop (or as full-screen apps in Tablet mode)

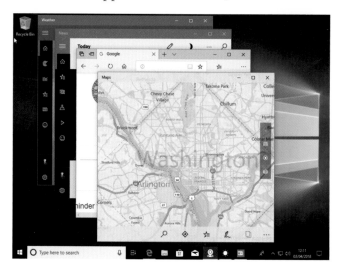

2 Click the Title bar on one app and drag it to the side of the screen, and release the mouse button when a frame appears showing the new location

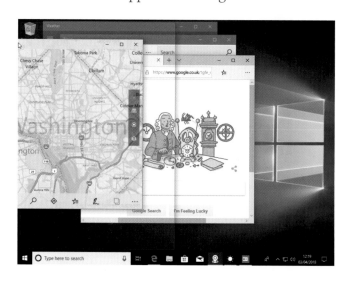

Don't forget

The minimum screen resolution to use the Windows 10 Snap feature is 1024 x 768, but it is more effective at higher resolutions.

Hot tip

In Tablet mode, move the mouse pointer to the top of the screen to reveal the app's Title bar, then click and drag this to the side.

On a touchscreen, drag the top edge down to reveal the Title bar.

Don't forget

You can select an app and press WinKey + Left arrow or WinKey + Right arrow to split the screen, then select the second app for the other half.

3 The other apps are displayed in Task View style on the other half of the screen. Select the app to be displayed in that half

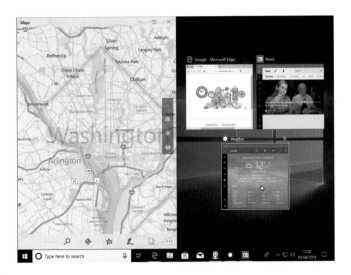

4 To arrange four apps on the screen, click on the Title bar of each app in turn and drag it to a corner

If you have a dual monitor system, you can have sets of two or more apps displayed on each monitor.

With two apps displayed, click and drag their edges to vary the share of the screen each one uses.

In Tablet mode, there's a divider between the two apps. Click and drag this bar to widen one app (and narrow the other).

41

You can position apps in corners using the keyboard. Press WinKey + Left arrow then Up arrow for the upper-left corner. For the other corners, use the (Right, Up), (Left, Down) and (Right, Down) combinations.

Close Apps

When apps are running in Desktop mode, they are windowed, and feature the Title bar with a Close button.

Apps not being displayed run in the background (if supported) or get suspended. This lets them restart quickly. You may prefer to explicitly close an app.

In Tablet mode, all apps run full-screen (except when you have Snap Assist in effect). Classic apps still show their Title bar and Close button, so you can easily end the app.

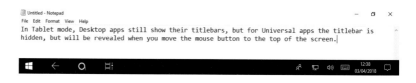

From the Taskbar, right-click the app icon and select Close window.

For Universal apps in Tablet mode, you need to reveal the Title bar and its Close button (see the Hot Tip on page 40), in order to end the app.

Alternatively, move the pointer over the icon until the thumbnail appears, then click the Close button.

You can also close any app in any mode by selecting the app and then pressing Alt + F4. Another option is to click and drag down (or touch and swipe down) the app screen until it shrinks and moves down to the bottom of the screen, then release it to close the app.

3 Windows 10 Desktop

Although the Start menu now features tiles, and touchscreen PCs can run in Tablet mode, Windows 10 still supports the windowed Desktop environment, including the Taskbar, Notification area, and the familiar windows structure, menus and dialogs for managing Desktop applications.

Desktop Mode

Switch on your computer to start up Windows 10 and display the Lock screen (see page 28), and then sign in to your user account. In most cases, the system will start up in Desktop mode, with no Start menu displayed.

The appearance of your Desktop will vary depending on configuration and personalization, but you should find:

Hot tip

To define an app that opens on your Desktop when you sign in, press WinKey + R, then type "shell:startup" and press Enter, to open your Startup folder. Drag and drop an entry from the All Apps list (see page 54) into this folder.

Don't forget

Touch-enabled PCs may start up in Tablet mode with the Start menu displayed full-screen, and no Desktop. However, these systems can also be set to start up in, or switch to, Desktop mode (see page 35).

Desktop Icons   Active Task   Background Image

Start Button   Cortana/Search Box   Taskbar Shortcuts   Active Task   Notification Area

The Touch keyboard button appears on the Taskbar for computers with touch-enabled monitors attached.

Touch Keyboard   Touch Keyboard Button

...cont'd

In Windows 10, all apps run on the Desktop; Universal as well as Classic Windows apps. To see how these appear:

1 Start a number of apps from the Start menu (see page 38) including, for example, some Office apps

If you have numerous apps open at once, you can organize them onto separate Desktops:

2 Select the Task View button, click New Desktop, then move some apps from Desktop 1 to Desktop 2

Task View Button

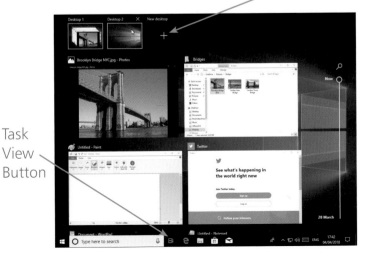

Hot tip

Right-click the Taskbar and select Cascade windows to organize all the open apps.

Hot tip

Right-click an app in Task View, click Move to, and choose the Desktop (or drag and drop an app onto the selected Desktop).

The Taskbar and Task View will show the apps that are on each of the Desktops.

45

Taskbar

The contents of the Taskbar change dynamically to reflect the activities that are taking place on your Desktop.

Taskbar Shortcuts

At the left of the Taskbar is the Start button, Cortana Search box, Task View and app shortcuts that turn into Task buttons (see below) when you run the apps – Microsoft Edge, File Explorer and the Microsoft Store, plus those you pin here.

Task Buttons (App Icons)

There is a Task button for each active task. The selected, or foreground task, in this case the Photos app, is shown emphasized. The blue underscore indicates activity:

One window – foreground, background

Two plus windows – foreground, background

Notification Area

The right-hand portion of the Taskbar is the Notification area, and contains Network, Speaker, Touch keyboard, Action Center and Date/Time. These are all system functions that are loaded automatically as Windows starts.

If there is more than one input language set on your system, there's a Language icon that lists the languages installed and allows you to switch.

Tablet Mode Taskbar

In Tablet mode, the Taskbar does not usually have the active task icons. To add them, right-click the Taskbar and select Show app icons.

...cont'd

If you start more tasks, the Taskbar may become full. Scrolling arrows will then be added to let you search for a specific task.

You can resize the Taskbar to show more apps at the same time, but first you may need to unlock it.

1 Right-click the Taskbar and, if there's a check next to Lock the taskbar, click that entry to remove the check and unlock the Taskbar

2 Move the mouse over the edge of the Taskbar until the pointer becomes a double-headed arrow, then drag the border up or down to resize the Taskbar

3 You can lock the Taskbar at the new size – reselect the Lock the taskbar option from the Taskbar right-click menu

You can also add other toolbars to the Taskbar:

1 Right-click an empty part of the Taskbar and select Toolbars

2 Select a toolbar entry and a tick will be added, and the toolbar will be displayed on the Taskbar. Reselect the toolbar entry to remove it

The Taskbar Settings entry gives options for customizing the location, operation and appearance of the Taskbar (see page 48). These were previously managed via Taskbar Properties in the Control Panel.

47

This right-click menu is also used to arrange windows and to open Task Manager, etc.

Taskbar Properties

To make changes to the Taskbar properties:

1 Right-click an empty part of the Taskbar and click Taskbar settings, to open at Personalization, Taskbar

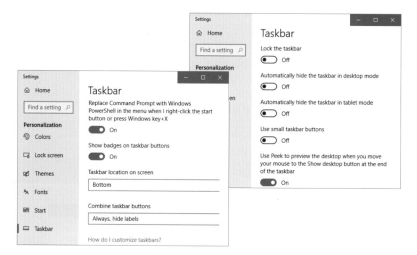

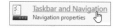
2 Scroll the list to see more options for the Taskbar

3 You can lock and unlock the Taskbar from Settings as well as from the right-click menu (see page 47)

4 Click the Automatically hide the taskbar button to On, to make the full area of the screen available to app windows

5 The Taskbar then reappears when you move the mouse to the part of the screen where the Taskbar would otherwise have been located

You can hide the Taskbar in Desktop mode or Tablet mode.

...cont'd

Small Taskbar Buttons

1 In Taskbar Settings, click Use small taskbar buttons On, so you can fit more items onto the Taskbar

Taskbar Location

1 Click the box labeled Taskbar location on screen, to display the options and reset the default location; e.g. Bottom goes to Top

Left
Top
Right
Bottom

Combine Taskbar Buttons

The default in Windows 10 is to show the Taskbar buttons without labels and to combine windows of the same type. However, you can keep things more separate.

1 Click the box for Combine taskbar buttons to display the options, and click When taskbar is full, and this will also show task labels

Always, hide labels
When taskbar is full
Never

2 Task labels may get truncated, and multiple tasks for a particular app may be combined on one button

3 With the Never option, task labels may be truncated or dropped, and Taskbar scrolling may be used

Hot tip

If the Taskbar is locked, there is no need to unlock the Taskbar when you want to change the size or its location on the screen.

49

Don't forget

This style of Taskbar works best on higher resolution screens, or with smaller numbers of active tasks.

Notification Area

The Notification area (previously called the System Tray) is at the right-hand side of the Taskbar. Some icons will appear by default, and installed programs may add icons. To control what is shown:

1 Open Taskbar settings (see page 48) and scroll down to the Notification area

Don't forget

The System icons that are offered depend on the configuration. For example, Network requires some form of connection, and Power is for laptop PCs only.

2 Pick Select which icons appear on the taskbar, and click Always show all icons in the notification area On, or set app icons On or Off individually

3 From the Settings in Step 1, choose Turn system icons on or off, and set each icon as desired

4 To manage the Notifications themselves, open Settings, select System and then select Notifications & actions

Don't forget

You can also choose which quick actions you want to appear in the Action Center (see page 227).

5 Choose to Get notifications from apps and other senders, and Show notifications on the lock screen

6 Specify when to Hide notifications

Peek At or Show Desktop

On the Taskbar to the right of the Notification area is the Show Desktop button. Starting with several open windows:

Peek is active only when you enable the option Use Peek to preview, from the Taskbar Settings (see page 48).

1 Hover over the Show Desktop button to see the Desktop, icons and outlines of all open windows

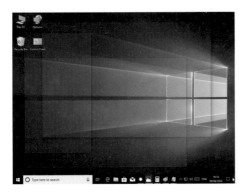

The Desktop and the outlines are displayed only temporarily, and the original window contents are redisplayed as soon as the mouse moves away from the Show Desktop button.

2 Click the Show Desktop button to hide the windows (and outlines) and show only the Desktop and icons

The Desktop is fully cleared, allowing you, if desired, to select a Desktop icon. Click the Show Desktop button again to restore the open windows.

Desktop Icons

Shortcuts to standard Windows applications can be stored on the Desktop. To start with, there are standard system icons:

1 To display or resize icons on the Desktop, right-click an empty part of the Desktop and select View

Don't forget

You can change the Desktop icons from the default size Medium, to Large as shown here, or to Small. You can also change their size by pressing the Ctrl button and scrolling the mouse wheel.

2 If the entry Show desktop icons is not already selected (ticked), then click to enable it

3 To specify which system icons to display, select Personalize from the right-click menu, and then Themes, Desktop icon settings

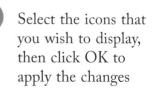

Don't forget

Click the Change Icon... button to select alternative images for any of the system icons. Click Restore Default to revert to the original images.

4 Select the icons that you wish to display, then click OK to apply the changes

For quick access, you can add shortcuts to the Taskbar for
both Classic and Universal apps:

1 Select the Search box on
the Taskbar and type an app
name; e.g. Notepad.exe

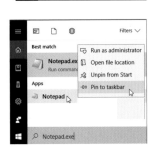

2 Right-click the result to
display the context menu
and select Pin to taskbar

3 View the Taskbar and you'll
see a new shortcut for the app

You can now run the app from the Taskbar. However, if
you prefer, you can create the app shortcut on the Desktop,
where there's more room for such shortcuts:

1 Right-click the search result
as above, and select Open
file location

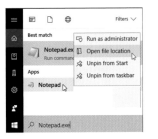

2 File Explorer opens with the
app file selected

3 Right-click the app file and
select Create shortcut

4 You are told that the shortcut
cannot be created here.
Confirm that the shortcut is
to be placed on the Desktop

5 You can now run that app from the Desktop
by double-clicking the shortcut icon

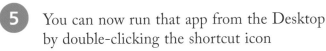

You can also right-click
the entry for the app
in the All Apps list and
select More to find Pin
to taskbar.

Similarly, you can use
All Apps to Open file
location for the app.

Open file location
appears only for
Classic apps. You need
to use the drag and
drop method (see
page 54) for Universal
app shortcuts.

...cont'd

You can also create shortcuts on the Desktop using drag and drop (see page 100) from the All Apps list, for both Classic and Universal apps.

1 Scroll to an app in the All Apps list, for example the Character Map in Windows Accessories

2 Select and drag the app icon onto the Desktop, and release it when the Link flag appears

3 Similarly, scroll to a Universal app such as Weather, and drag and drop it onto the Desktop

You can add other Windows Accessories such as Paint and Notepad (see pages 110-112), applications such as Word and Excel from the Microsoft Office suite, and Universal apps such as Money.

You can drag the Desktop shortcut icons to arrange them in groups according to type, perhaps, or by project or activity.

Note that Universal app shortcuts do not display live updates, as featured with the app tiles on the Start menu.

Don't forget

You can right-click the Taskbar shortcut for any app you've now added to the Desktop, and select Unpin from taskbar to remove the link to that app.

Hot tip

You may also find that some applications automatically get shortcuts added to the Desktop when installed; for example, Adobe Reader.

Window Structure

When you open a folder, or start a Windows function or application program on the Desktop, it appears as a window that can be moved and resized. For example:

 Click the File Explorer shortcut icon on the Taskbar

Not all the Windows applications use the Ribbon style. See page 56 for Notepad, an example of a conventional window.

Features of the Window

Quick Access Toolbar

Forward and Back Arrows

Ribbon

Minimize and Maximize Buttons

Close Button

Command Bar

Search Box

Address Bar

Contents Pane

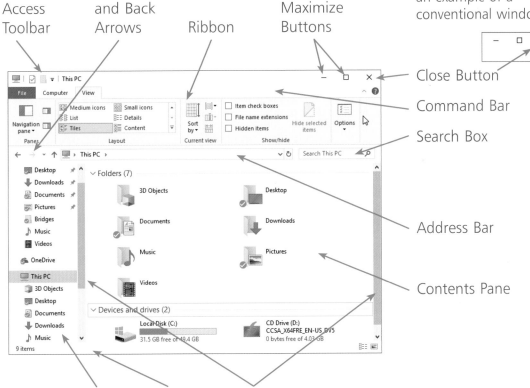

Navigation Pane

Status Bar

Scroll Bars

 Click the Maximize button to view the window using the whole screen, and the Restore button appears in place of it

Application Windows

Application programs, even the ones included in Windows 10, may still use the traditional window structure, with a Title bar and Menu bar. For example, the Notepad application window:

1 Select Start, Windows Accessories, then Notepad, then type some text (or open an existing file)

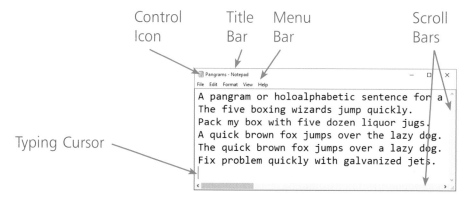

Control Icon   Title Bar   Menu Bar   Scroll Bars

Typing Cursor

Other Windows 10 applications such as WordPad and Paint use the Scenic Ribbon in place of the Menu bar.

1 Select Start, Windows Accessories, then WordPad, and then open a file (or type some text)

Some applications may not use all the features; e.g. Character Map uses a window with no scroll bars, and cannot be resized.

File Tab   Quick Access Toolbar   Tabs   Ribbon

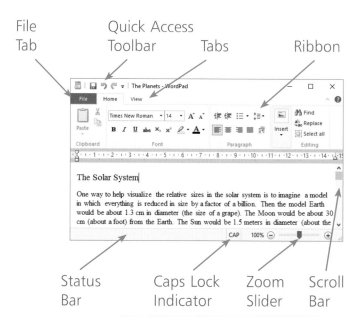

Status Bar   Caps Lock Indicator   Zoom Slider   Scroll Bar

Menus and Dialogs

The entries on the Command bars, Menu bars and Ribbons expand to provide a list of related options to choose. Some entries expand into a sub-menu; for example:

1 Open the Libraries folder (see page 96), select Documents and click Manage, then click Set save location. Note the sub-menu for Set public save location

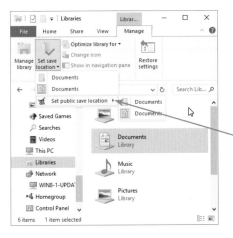

Other commands open dialog boxes that allow you to apply more complex configurations and settings. For example:

1 Select a library as above, select the Home tab, and then click the Properties button

2 The Properties panel is displayed

3 Make changes and click Apply then OK to confirm, or click Restore Defaults to undo

Beware

If a library has only one folder, Set save location is grayed out. To add folders to a library, select Manage, and click the Library button.

Don't forget

The black triangle next to a menu entry indicates that there are additional options available to be displayed.

Hot tip

Some entries are toggles that switch on when selected, then switch off when reselected. For example, a ✓ symbol, may be added to or removed from a box.

Move and Resize Windows

Double-clicking on the Title bar has the same effect as the Maximize and Restore buttons.

To show a frame as you drag a window, open the System panel (see page 11), select Advanced System Settings, click the Settings button for Performance, then select Adjust.

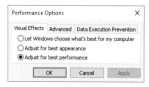

Dragging a corner of the window allows you to adjust the two adjacent borders at the same time.

1 To maximize the window, double-click the Title bar area (double-click again to restore the window to its original size)

2 To move the window, click the Title bar area, hold down the mouse button and drag the window

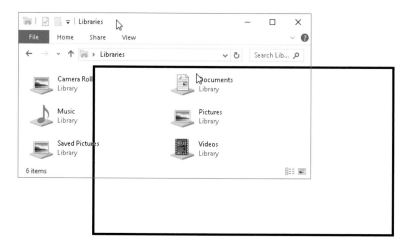

3 To resize the window, move the mouse pointer over any border or any corner

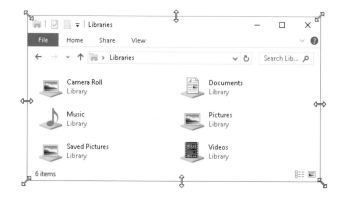

4 When the double-headed resize arrow appears, click and drag until the window is the desired size

Snap Assist

On the Windows 10 Desktop, the Snap Assist feature offers ways to move and resize windows in one movement.

Maximize the Window

1 Drag the Title bar to the top of the screen

2 The window's outline expands to fill the whole Desktop

3 Release the Title bar to maximize the window

Expand Vertically

1 Drag the top border of the window to the top of the screen

2 The window's outline expands to the height of the Desktop

3 Release the mouse to maximize the height but maintain the width of the window

Half or Quarter Screen

You can move the Classic app window to the side or corner.

1 Drag the Title bar to the left or right edge and release it there after the half-screen outline appears, for a half screen

2 Drag the Title bar to any corner and release it there once the quarter-screen outline has appeared, for a quarter screen

Don't forget

You can also drag the bottom border to the bottom edge, to expand the window vertically.

Hot tip

To return the dragged window to its previous size and position, just double-click on the Title bar.

Hot tip

In Tablet mode, all app windows are full-screen. They can be minimized but cannot be resized, except via the Snap Assist options (see pages 40-41).

Don't forget

You can make the Start menu full-screen via Settings. Open Personalization and select Start, then turn on the toggle for Use Start full screen.

This will look like Tablet mode, but you'll still have support for both Classic and Universal apps.

Universal Windows Apps

When you are working in Desktop mode, the windows for your Universal apps operate just like those for Classic apps, with Cascade, Resize, Minimize, Maximize and Close, etc.

However, there is a minimum size for most apps; e.g. the Weather app can be no less than 502 x 353 pixels.

Start Menu

The Start menu panel operates like a window, but with limitations. There's a vertical scroll bar, and you can drag the top and right edges, but the panel resizes in stages. The bottom-left corner is fixed in position, and there's no Title bar and no Minimize, Maximize or Close buttons.

4 Personalize Your System

In this chapter you will learn how to change the appearance of the Windows 10 Lock screen and Start menu, add an account picture, organize the tiles and the apps, manage your user account, add a picture password or PIN code, and take advantage of ease of use features. You can also personalize the Desktop environment and manage the display options, including screen resolution and multiple displays.

You can also open Settings by clicking All settings in the Action Center (see page 32).

Press WinKey + X, or scroll the All Apps list and find Windows System, Control Panel. See page 78 for more ways to open the Control Panel.

Settings

Windows 10 provides the Settings function to make changes to your system, and (if you use a Microsoft Account) you can apply those changes when you sign in to a different PC.

There are several ways to open Settings:

1 Select Settings from the column of icons at the left of the Start menu

2 Select Settings from the alphabetic All Apps list

3 Press WinKey + I to open Settings

4 Open File Explorer (see page 94), select This PC; then the Computer tab; and click the Open Settings button on the Ribbon

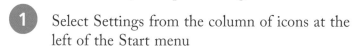

Windows 10 still uses the Control Panel, as used in previous versions of Windows, for changing some settings.

Personalize Lock Screen

The Lock screen appears when you start Windows 10, sign out, or resume from Sleep. To customize this screen:

1 Open Settings (see previous page), click Personalization and then select Lock screen

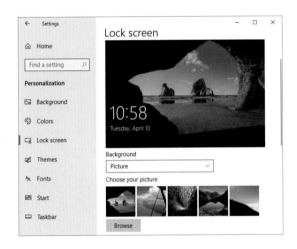

2 Scroll down and select one of the supplied pictures to make it the background image

3 Alternatively, click Browse to select an image from your Pictures library or from a different image folder

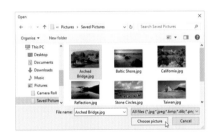

4 Scroll further down the Lock screen settings pane to choose apps that can display live notifications, updates, a quick status, or alarms

Don't forget

You can also open Personalization by right-clicking the Desktop and selecting Personalize. (The spellings are localized depending on the language selected in Settings.)

Hot tip

You can also choose to display the contents of your Pictures library as a slideshow on the Lock screen.

Don't forget

You can have a single app giving detailed updates, plus up to seven Universal apps that provide quick status updates.

...cont'd

Hot tip

You don't have to save the changes or close the Settings function to apply the changes. The updates will be applied immediately.

5 Click the existing app icon or the Add (+) icon and select the desired app that will display a detailed status or alarms (or select None to remove a selection)

6 Similarly, you can choose apps to show a quick status (or select None to remove a selection)

You can view your changes to the Lock screen immediately. To do this:

1 Switch to the Start menu and right-click the user icon on the Start menu

2 Select Lock to display the Lock screen, whilst still retaining your session (but not Sign out, since that ends the session)

Don't forget

You will have status indicators in the form of icons; e.g. Network for connected PCs and Power for battery PCs.

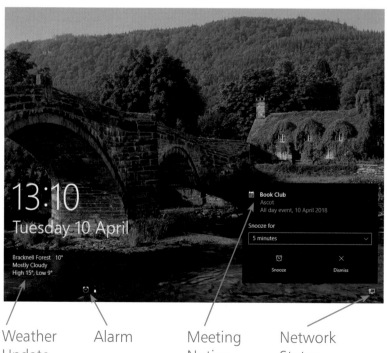

Weather Update   Alarm   Meeting Notice   Network Status

Desktop

1 Open Settings, click Personalization and then select Background

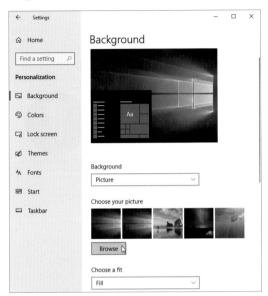

2 Choose Picture from the drop-down menu and select an image to act as the background for the Desktop

3 You can also click Browse and select an image from your Pictures library or another image folder

4 Select Start, to control what items are on the left-hand side of the Start menu

5 Select Colors, to apply a color accent to the Taskbar, window borders and the Start menu

6 Select Fonts, to display the fonts available on your system, and get more fonts from the Microsoft Store

7 Select Themes, to apply predefined sets of colors, images and sound effects, and other related settings

Don't forget

The background can be a picture, a slideshow or simply a solid color. The image may fill the screen; fit to height; stretch both ways; tile; center; or span across multiple monitors.

65

Hot tip

Select Show more tiles to have four columns of tiles rather than three.

Beware

If you are signed in with a Microsoft Account, your choices will be applied to any Windows 10 PC you sign in to with that Microsoft Account.

Account Picture

You can specify a photo or image that will be used alongside your username on the Start menu:

1 Open Settings and select Accounts, or right-click the username on the Start menu screen and select Change account settings, then click Your info

You can select or create a picture of any size, and it will be converted to the appropriate size for use with the Start menu or other functions related to your Microsoft Account.

Make sure you select a square image, as you can't crop or move the image once you have selected it as your Microsoft Account photo.

2 Click Browse for one to select an existing photo or other image from your Pictures library or another folder

3 Alternatively, if your computer has a webcam or built-in camera, select Camera to take a picture

4 You can take a still photo or a video, but the video is limited to five seconds

5 Press the Windows key to toggle between the Settings screen and Start menu, to see the results

You can change the user image from any Windows 10 PC, but to remove it completely you may need to sign in to your Microsoft Account using a web browser and amend your profile there.

If you are signed in with a Microsoft Account, the selected image will be displayed on the Start menu of any Windows 10 computer that you sign in to.

Manage Tiles

The app tiles displayed on your Start menu will depend on the choices made by the manufacturer or supplier of your computer, and may be in no particular order or sequence. However, you have full control and can resize, rearrange, remove and add tiles as it suits you.

Choose Tiles

The first task is to choose a tile. You can't just click or touch it, since that will run the associated program. Instead:

1 To choose a tile with the mouse, right-click the tile and the context menu appears

2 Select the required action, or click Resize to see the options

The actions offered depend on the particular app selected. For Money, you can Unpin from Start, Resize, Turn live tile off (or back on), Pin to taskbar (or Unpin) and Uninstall.

You can choose from up to four sizes of tile – three square sizes (Large, Medium and Small) and one oblong size (Wide). For some Universal apps, the choice is more limited, and even more so for Classic applications; for example:

1 Select a Universal app such as Search and you'll see three tile sizes offered – Small, Medium and Wide

2 Select another Universal app such as Settings and you may see just Medium and Small sizes, as you do for any Classic app; e.g. Access

With a touchscreen, touch and hold the tile, to access buttons to Unpin and More options. Touch the latter to see all the actions offered.

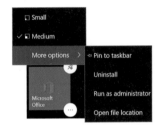

Don't forget

Select and hold a tile and drag it into a new position, and the tiles will automatically reflow. This will also happen when you Unpin or Resize tiles.

Don't forget

As always, the options offered vary depending on the type of entry selected and its current status.

Hot tip

Click the Expand arrow next to an entry, for example Windows Accessories, to show all the items it includes.

68

...cont'd

3 Right-click the Microsoft Store app to see the actions that are offered for this Universal app

You can Unpin from Start, Resize, Turn live tile off or Unpin from taskbar or App settings, but there's no Uninstall.

Add Tiles

The All Apps list is the usual place to locate apps and add their tiles to the Start menu.

1 In Desktop mode, select Start (if Expand is in effect) to show the All Apps column

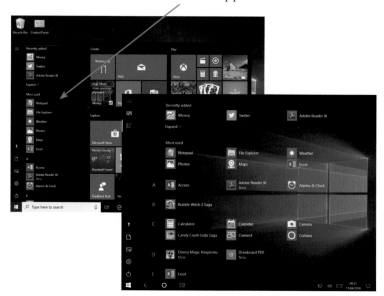

2 For Full Screen Start or in Tablet mode, select All apps to show three columns of apps

You'll see all the Universal and Classic apps that are installed on your system, listed alphabetically by name. Some apps are grouped in folders, for example Windows Accessories, Windows Ease of Access and Windows System, plus Microsoft Office Tools (if installed). Any other apps or programs that you subsequently download and install will also be included in the list.

Manage Apps

Select Universal or Classic apps of different types to see what actions are offered:

1 Select a Universal app that's currently on the Start menu and you can Unpin from Start, Pin to taskbar or Uninstall

2 For a Universal app not currently on the Start menu, you can Pin to Start, Pin to taskbar or Uninstall

3 Select a Windows Accessory such as Paint and you can Pin to Start, Pin to taskbar, Run as administrator or Open file location

4 If the Windows Accessory or Classic app is already pinned to Start, you get Unpin from Start, Pin to taskbar, Uninstall, Run as administrator and Open file location

5 You can right-click any entry in the Most used or Recently added sections of the Start menu, where you'll see the additional option: Don't show in this list

You can find out how many apps you have in your system:

1 Run Windows PowerShell and enter the command **Get-StartApps | measure** and the total number of apps will be displayed

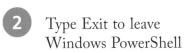

2 Type Exit to leave Windows PowerShell

Don't forget

You can add items from the Desktop to the Start menu, such as disks, libraries and folders. Right-click the item in File Explorer and select Pin to Start from the menu.

69

Hot tip

Type "Powershell" in the Search box and press Enter, or locate Windows PowerShell in the All Apps list, and run the app.

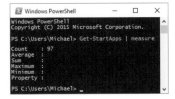

Create a Group

Only some of the apps on your system are included as tiles on the Start menu, so you must add any others you want. You can arrange them in groups so they are easy to locate:

When you add new apps from the Store, or install applications such as Microsoft Office, they are added to the All Apps list, but no tiles are added to the Start menu.

1 Select each Windows Accessory or Office app in turn, and choose Pin to Start

When you pin apps to the Start menu, their tiles will be added to the right of existing tiles, or below them, as space permits.

2 The apps you pin are added after the existing apps, with no automatic grouping

3 To create a group for the Accessories, select one of them and begin to drag it towards an empty space

Hot tip

When you drag the tile, make sure to keep it away from existing groups, otherwise it could get added to one of them rather than creating a new group. To correct any misplaced tiles, simply reselect and redrag.

4 When the bar appears, release the tile to drop it into the new group

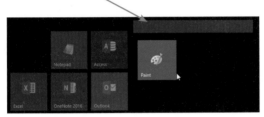

5 Drag and drop other Accessories into the new group

6 We now have two groups, one for Office and one for Accessories, though at this point neither is named

Name the Group

1 Point and hover or Touch above the group and the Name group option is displayed

2 Click Name group, and a typing area is presented

3 Type a name for the group, e.g. Windows Accessories, and click an empty part of the Start menu to apply the name

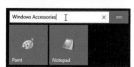

4 Repeat this procedure to add the name for the other group; i.e. Microsoft Office 2016

5 There are now Group name headers for both groups

Hot tip

You can reorder (and resize) the tiles in a group, for example, by putting the most used apps at the top.

6 To change or delete a Group name, click in the Group name to reveal the typing area, make the change, and then press Enter

Change User Account

1   Open Settings, select Accounts, then Your info

2   If you are signed in with a Local Account, you can switch to a Microsoft Account instead

3   If you are signed in with a Microsoft Account, you can switch to a Local Account instead

4   In either case, you can change your password, create a picture password, create a PIN or add a new user

You'll be asked to provide an email address, which may be for an existing Microsoft Account, or one that can be used to create such an account.

You must provide a username, password and password hint to aid signing in to this computer. Note that as a Local Account, it will not be synced with your other Windows computers.

PIN is an acronym for Personal Identification Number, and is usually a four-digit code (see page 76 for options).

Picture Password

Don't forget

You'd normally use picture passwords with a touchscreen, but it is possible to use a mouse.

Don't forget

The picture password consists of three gestures, applied in sequence at specific locations. You can choose one or more types of gesture – draw a circle, draw a straight line or tap the screen at a point.

Hot tip

If needed, you can start over to enter a new set of gestures, if you are having trouble repeating your initial selection.

1 Open Settings, select Accounts, then Sign-in options, and then Add underneath Picture password

2 Type your password to verify the account, then click OK

3 Select Choose picture, find a suitable picture file, then click Open

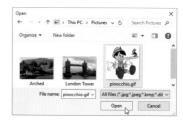

4 Follow the prompts to position the picture, draw the three gestures and confirm your gestures

...cont'd

5 When you've successfully confirmed your gestures and your picture password is set up, click Finish

The selected gestures – a circle, a line and a tap – are shown here for illustration purposes, but such indicators will not normally appear on the display, except when you are having problems during the initial setup.

The next time the Lock screen appears and you sign in, you'll be able to use your picture password.

You can use Windows Hello to sign in if your PC is set up for it. Go to Start, select Settings, Accounts and Sign-in options. Under Windows Hello, you'll see options for face, fingerprint or iris, if your PC has a fingerprint reader or a camera that supports it. Once you're set up, you'll be able to use Windows Hello to sign in.

6 If you wish, you can select Sign-in options to switch to the normal password sign-in procedure

PIN Code

76

1 Open Settings, select Accounts, then Sign-in options, and then select Add (underneath PIN)

2 Enter your password to verify your account and click Sign in

3 Enter four or more digits for the PIN and re-enter the numbers to confirm the PIN code

4 On a tablet PC, select the entry box for the PIN, to display the touch keypad for numeric entry

5 Select OK when the values have been entered

When you next sign in, you'll be asked for the PIN, which you can enter by keyboard or touch. Just provide the four digits – there's no need for the Enter key.

Click Sign-in options if you want to switch between the picture password, your Microsoft Account password, and the PIN code. All three are valid.

Ease of Access

Windows 10 Settings also allow you to set up Ease of Access options on your computer, to improve accessibility.

1 Open Settings, select Ease of Access and review the categories listed

2 Select Magnifier to turn Magnifier on, invert colors and enable tracking (to have Magnifier follow the keyboard focus or the mouse cursor)

3 Select Mouse to adjust the pointer size, change the pointer color or use the numeric keypad to move the mouse around the screen

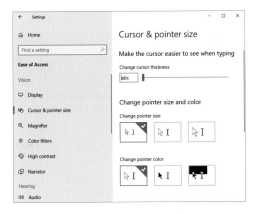

4 You can also manage use of the screen, keyboard and other options such as cursor thickness

You'll find help and guidance for using the options in the Ease of Access Center in the Control Panel (see page 82), or click Get help in Settings, Ease of Access.

To make the typing cursor easier to spot, select Other options then drag the slider for Cursor thickness until it is the size you'd like.

Select Narrator to turn on the screen reader for text and controls; choose a voice; select sounds; and manage keyboard and mouse actions.

77

Open Control Panel

In previous versions of Windows, the most comprehensive options for customizing your system were provided via the Control Panel. Although the Settings feature is gradually taking over, the Control Panel is still important, so there are several ways to access this:

Hot tip

Select Windows System, Control Panel from the All Apps list. Another option is to press the WinKey + R keys to open the Run command box, type "Control Panel" and then click OK.

1 From the Start menu Search box, start typing Control Panel. When the Control Panel entry appears, click it or press Enter

2 From the Desktop, with Show desktop icons enabled (see page 52), double-click the Control Panel icon (if that icon is enabled for display)

Beware

In initial versions of Windows 10 you could open the Control Panel from the Power User menu (see page 36). However this entry is no longer offered in the latest versions.

3 Open File Explorer from the Taskbar, or the Start menu, select This PC and then click the Up arrow to go up a folder level to Desktop

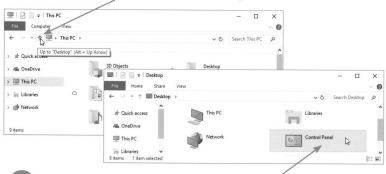

4 In the Desktop folder, select the Control Panel entry

Personalize via Control Panel

Some options for personalizing the Desktop are still found in the Control Panel. To personalize your system:

1 Select the Appearance and Personalization option (when the Control Panel is displayed in View by: Categories)

Control Panel options are still used to adjust settings for File Explorer and to manage fonts.

2 Select File Explorer Options to manage how you access files and folders with this application

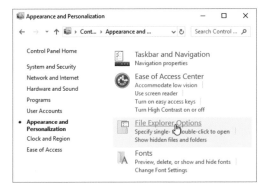

3 Select the General tab to control how you browse folders, use single- or double-click, and manage Privacy settings

Other changes to the Desktop such as background and color must be made through the Settings app (see pages 62 and 65).

4 You can also adjust Folder View and Search options

Display Settings

1 Right-click the desktop and select Display settings

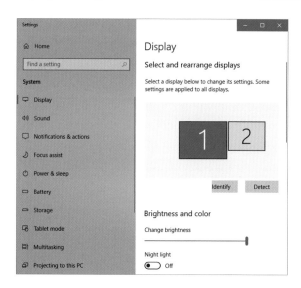

You can type "display" in the Search box and select Change display settings when this result appears (or open Settings, select System, and then Display).

2 Select a display (if more than one), adjust brightness, turn on Night light, or scroll down for more options

Screens emit blue light, which may be less comfortable at night, so you can turn on Night light so the screen will display warmer colors.

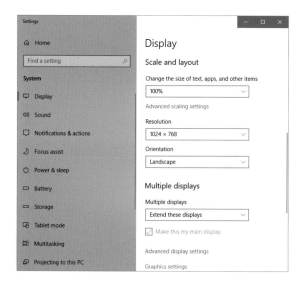

3 A scaling factor for text and apps will be recommended, but you can change this if desired

...cont'd

4 Click the Resolution box to see the alternatives available

5 Choose the new resolution that you want to use, if the recommendation doesn't suit

The higher the resolution, the more you can fit on the screen, but the smaller the text and images that will then appear.

6 Click the Orientation box to select Landscape or Portrait. These can be flipped if appropriate

7 If you have multiple displays, select how they will be used

You can duplicate the screen contents, extend to use both (one being the main display), or just use a single screen.

Any adjustments to Night light or Scaling will be applied immediately, but when revisions of any other settings are applied, you will be asked to confirm that you want to keep the changes you have made.

> **Keep these display settings?**
> Reverting to previous display settings in 6 seconds.
>
> Keep changes   Revert

8 If you want to retain the display settings as shown, you should click Keep changes

To cancel the changes, you'd select Revert, or simply leave the system alone, and after 15 seconds the changes are undone.

The screen thumbnails will change to reflect the resolution and orientation changes. You can also drag and drop the thumbnails to match the physical arrangement.

The resolutions, color settings and connections offered depend on the type of monitor and the type of graphics adapter that you have on your computer.

Ease of Access Center

Hot tip

If your PC has a microphone attached, you can use it for Speech Recognition, to dictate to the computer, or to issue commands to control the computer.

Don't forget

The magnifier is not just for text; it is also very useful for close-up views of images of all types, including graphics, buttons and pictures.

Hot tip

Scroll down the settings and select Make the mouse easier to use, and you can turn on mouse keys and the numeric keypad to move the mouse around the screen.

1 From the Control Panel select the Ease of Access category

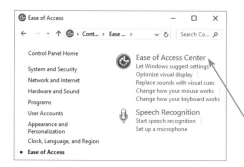

2 For an explanation of the options available, select the green Ease of Access Center link

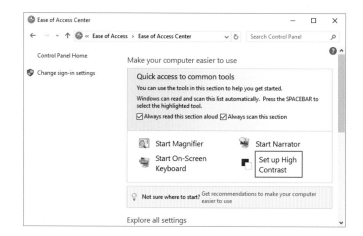

3 Start the main tools – Magnifier, Narrator, On-Screen Keyboard, High Contrast

4 If you are unsure, you can ask for recommendations to make your computer easier to use

5 Scroll down to explore settings, to optimize the computer for limited vision, to set up alternatives for input devices and sound, and to make touch easier to use

5 Search and Organize

Windows 10 helps organize the files and folders on your hard disk. Data is stored by username with separate folders for different types of files, or you can add new folders. Libraries allow you to work with a group of folders. Powerful instant search facilities help you find your way around the folders and the menus.

Files and Folders

The hardware components are the building blocks for your computer, but it is the information on your hard disk that really makes your computer operate. There is a huge number of files and folders stored there. To get an idea of how many:

1 In the Search box on the Taskbar, type Computer and click This PC from the results

2 In the File Explorer window that appears, double-click the Local Disk (C:) to open it

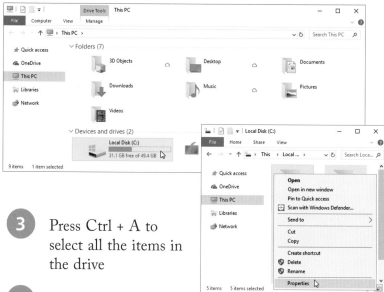

3 Press Ctrl + A to select all the items in the drive

4 Right-click the selection and click Properties

5 This example shows totals of almost 100,000 files and over 22,000 folders on the C: drive

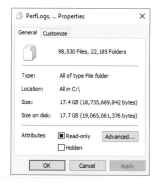

84

...cont'd

With so many files and folders to handle, they must be well organized to ensure that you can locate the documents, pictures and other data that you require with ease. Windows helps by grouping the files into related sections, for example:

- Program Files   Application programs (64-bit)
- Program Files (x86)   Application programs (32-bit)
- Program Data   Application data files (hidden)
- Windows   Operating system files & data
- Users   Documents, pictures, etc.

These are top-level folders on your hard disk and each one is divided into sub-folders. For example, the Program Files folders are arranged by supplier and application.

1 Open the C: drive, then double-click Program Files, (x86) then Adobe and then the Reader sub-folders

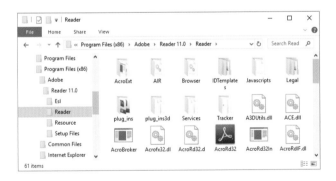

2 Move the mouse pointer over the Navigation pane and you'll see arrows next to some folders

3 The gray arrow symbol (>) shows there are sub-folders within that folder

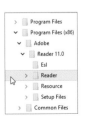

The black symbol (⌄) means that the folder is at least partially expanded

On a 32-bit Windows system there is just the Program Files folder, which then holds 32-bit programs such as Adobe Reader.

85

The Users folder contains Documents, Pictures, Music and other folders for each user defined on the computer.

The gray and black arrow symbols also appear when you select any of the folder names within the Navigation pane.

New User Account

Hot tip

You can add other users as part of your family group, giving them an account of their own with libraries and standard folders.

Don't forget

If the new user does not already have a Microsoft Account, you can create one as part of the process of adding the user's account.

Hot tip

Adults added to your family group can manage the settings for the children in the group.

1 Open Settings (see page 62), select Accounts and then select Family & other people, then click the Add a family member button

2 Select Add an adult, and provide the email address for the person's Microsoft Account

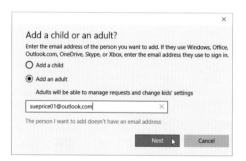

3 Click Next, and follow the prompts to invite that user to join your family group and set the account up on the system, ready for sign-in

4 Add a child to your family group

As with the adult, an invitation to join the group is sent as an email, and the child's account is made ready for sign-in.

Any new users that you create are added to the Family & other people section of the Accounts settings.

5 You can also add someone else to the PC, although not as a member of your family group, so no invitation will be issued

You can allow a new user to sign in while you are still logged on to the computer:

6 From the Start menu, click the current user and select the new user

7 From the Sign-in screen that appears, type the password and press Enter

If you sign out, switch user or shut down/restart, the new username can be selected from the Sign-in screen.

Windows creates the user libraries and folders (see pages 92-96), and installs any necessary apps. Progress messages are displayed.

sueprice01@outlook.com

This won't take long

Setting up your apps

Setup completes, and Windows restarts with the new user account active.

87

Finalize New Account

Respond to Invitation

1 Open the invitation email sent to the new user and click the Accept Invitation button

Michael invited you to join their family

Microsoft Family (microsoftfamily@microsoft.com) ● Add to contacts 15:45
To:

■ Microsoft

Michael would like you to join their family as an adult.
If you accept, you'll be able to approve requests, change kids' settings and get weekly activity reports.

Accept Invitation

This invitation will expire in 14 days.

To learn more, visit http://account.microsoft.com/family

2 Click Sign in and join to confirm membership and view details of adult and child members

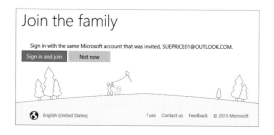

Join the family

Sign in with the same Microsoft account that was invited, SUEPRICE01@OUTLOOK.COM.

Sign in and join   Not now

● English (United States)   ┆use Contact us Feedback © 2015 Microsoft

Verify Your Account

1 Open Settings, Accounts, Your info and click Verify if so indicated

← Settings   — □ ×
⌂ Home

Find a setting   **SUE PRICE**
                  Billing info, family settings, subscriptions, security
Accounts   settings, and more
A≡ Your info   Manage my Microsoft account
                  You need to verify your identity on this PC.
🔍 Sign-in options   Verify

2 Give your contact details, and enter the security code that you'll be sent via the selected method

Verify email
We sent an email to your email address to make sure you own it. Please check your inbox and enter the security code below to finish setting up your Microsoft account.

••••••••   ✕

Didn't receive the email? Resend it now.   Next

Change Account Type

1 Open the Control Panel (View by: Category), and in the User Accounts category select Change account type

2 Select one of the new accounts

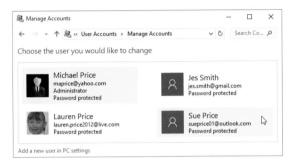

3 Select Change the account type and you'll see that it has been set as Standard

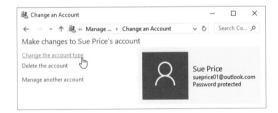

4 Select Cancel to exit without making any changes

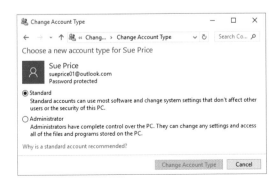

This displays details of all the accounts on your computer. You'll see that the first account, created when the system was originally set up, has been defined as Administrator.

You cannot create new accounts from within the Control Panel. You must select the Add a new user in PC settings link, at the bottom of the Manage Accounts screen.

Standard user accounts are recommended for every user, even the Administrator. To minimize the risk of unintended changes, Windows will ask for the Administrator password when that level is needed.

Set Up Assigned Access

Don't forget

With assigned access you can restrict an account so that it only has access to one Universal app. This is for using the PC for a predefined function only and is perhaps an alternative to the Guest user, which has been removed from Windows 10.

1 Open Settings and select Accounts, Family & other people and then Set up assigned access

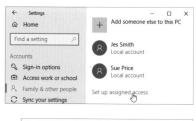

2 Click Choose an account and select one of the users from the list displayed

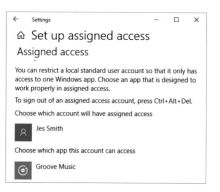

3 Click Choose an app and select the app that the user requires

4 Access to the specified app is now defined for the selected user

Don't forget

It isn't essential to restart your PC to apply the changes and make the newly assigned account available for use.

5 To try out the new access, sign out or restart the system so that it displays the Lock screen

...cont'd

6 Select or swipe up on the Lock screen to display Sign-in

7 Select the user with assigned access and enter the password

Any data that the app needs must be preloaded, as it isn't possible to run any other apps while the assigned access app is running, since there's no Taskbar, no Start menu and no way to switch apps.

8 The system starts up and the specified app is displayed, ready for use

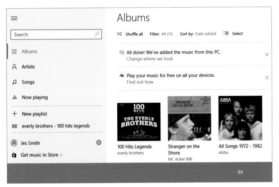

9 The Groove Music app, for example, will locate music on the system and make it ready to play

When you switch users from the user with assigned access and shut down, you may be told that there is still a user active, since you haven't explicitly signed out.

10 When the assigned access session is no longer required, you must enter Ctrl + Alt + Del to return to the Sign-in screen where you can shut down or switch users

User Folders

Documents and pictures that you create or save on your computer are kept in folders associated with your username.

The Public folder is available to all user accounts and can be used to share files with other people using the same computer or using other computers on the same network. To share with any internet-connected computer or device, use OneDrive (see pages 94-95).

1 Open the C: drive in File Explorer (see page 84) and double-click the Users folder

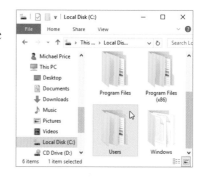

2 There's a sub-folder for each user account name, plus the Public folder

To see the hierarchical structure of the user folders, right-click the Navigation pane and select Expand to current folder.

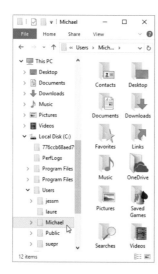

3 Double-click the folder for the active user, in this case Michael

There is a set of sub-folders with all the documents, pictures, data files and settings belonging to that user. There's also a link to OneDrive, the online storage for the user.

Each user folder (including the Public folder) has a similar set of sub-folders defined.

The Documents, Music, Pictures and Videos folders can be accessed from This PC in File Explorer, and also from the Libraries link that can be added to the Navigation pane (see page 97).

This PC

This PC in File Explorer is a new feature in Windows 10. Like the Computer entry from previous versions of Windows, it provides a list of the storage devices and drives attached to the local computer.

1 Open File Explorer and click This PC

2 The lower group shows the Devices and drives, in this case the disk drive and the CD drive

In addition, however, File Explorer lists some of the folders associated with the active user.

3 The upper group shows folders for the current user, including Documents, Music, Pictures and Videos (the same folders as used by Libraries)

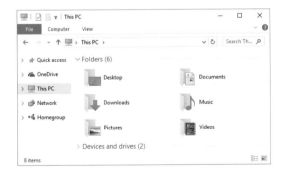

4 The Downloads and the Desktop folders are also listed in this group of folders

This PC replaces the Computer entry that you find in previous versions of Windows.

It also replaces (to an extent) the Libraries entry, though this can be reinstated (see page 96).

These are shortcuts, effectively linking to the actual folders on the hard disk of the PC.

OneDrive

OneDrive is Microsoft's Cloud storage that comes with your Microsoft Account. You can have up to 5GB storage free, and can access it from any device where you sign in with your Microsoft Account, or from any web browser. File Explorer gives local copies of folders kept in sync with your OneDrive:

Don't forget

The original feature was called SkyDrive but was renamed OneDrive for copyright reasons.

1 Open File Explorer and select OneDrive in the Navigation pane to see the OneDrive folders that are kept locally; e.g. Documents, Music, Pictures

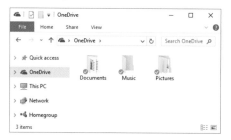

Don't forget

In previous versions of Windows, you needed a Classic app to access OneDrive. In Windows 10 you can use File Explorer to transfer files to and from OneDrive.

2 You can also click the OneDrive icon in the Notification area to Open your OneDrive folder

3 To select the files to sync, right-click the OneDrive icon and select Settings, then Choose folders on the Account tab

Hot tip

Only the folders you choose to sync will be shown in the local copy of OneDrive. Any changes you make are applied to the online OneDrive immediately, or the next time you connect to the internet.

There may be other folders on your OneDrive that are not shown on your local copy. If you choose another folder, it will be added and its contents copied. If you deselect a folder, it and all of its files are removed from the local copy.

94

...cont'd

4 Right-click the OneDrive icon and select Upgrade to see how much storage you have

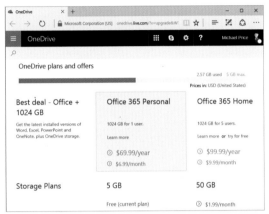

5 Microsoft gives you options to earn extra storage, or you can purchase additional blocks

If you are signed in with a Local Account, you may find OneDrive shown in File Explorer, but it will have no contents.

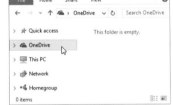

6 Select OneDrive from the Navigation pane, and you are invited to set up OneDrive. You'll need a Microsoft Account to complete the procedure

Hot tip

By default, you get 5GB of free OneDrive storage space with Windows 10 (the free allowance was reduced from 15GB in January 2016). This is an excellent way to back up your important documents, since they are stored away from your computer. For up-to-date information on plan allowances and pricing, visit **https://onedrive.live.com/about/plans/**

Beware

If you sign in with a Local Account, the OneDrive entry may appear in File Explorer, but you cannot access OneDrive folders unless you provide a Microsoft Account.

Libraries

Libraries contain shortcuts to individual folders but allow you to treat the contents as if they were all in one folder. Typically, the Documents library would be a combination of the user's Documents folder and the Public Documents folder. This allows you to share documents with others (or access their documents). In Windows 10, Libraries are not displayed by default, but you can add them to File Explorer.

Don't forget

You can right-click any folder on your hard disk or OneDrive, select Include in library and add it to any of your libraries, or use it to create a new library.

① Open File Explorer, right-click the Navigation pane and select the option to Show libraries

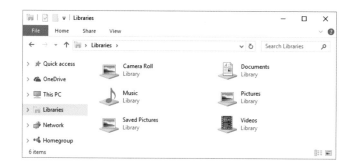

② Select the Libraries entry that gets added, and you'll see the expected four libraries – Documents, Pictures, Music and Videos plus, perhaps, Saved Pictures and Camera Roll, used by the Photos and Camera apps

③ Double-click the Documents library and you'll see it has files from two locations – the user's OneDrive Documents folder (local copy of online folder) and the user's local Documents folder

Hot tip

By default, your OneDrive is set up for sharing documents, though you can revert to the local Public folders if you wish to share files on your local area network only.

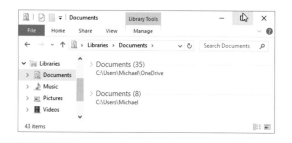

Folder Navigation

When you open a drive or folder, you'll find a number of different ways to navigate around the folders on your disk.

1 Open, for example, a sub-folder in Pictures using File Explorer

Quick Access Toolbar   Tab Bar   Title Bar   Search Box Help

Forward, Back

Up One Level

Address Bar

Navigation Pane

Contents Pane

Details Pane

Status Bar

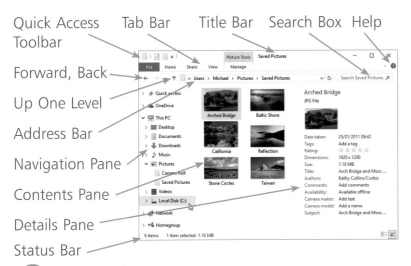

Click the Forward and Back arrows to navigate through locations you have already visited.

2 To go directly to a location on the Address bar, just click that location; for example the User's folder (in this case, Michael)

3 To go to a sub-folder of a location on the Address bar, click the arrow to the right of that location, and select a sub-folder from the list displayed

4 To type a location, click the blank space to the right of the current location

« Users › Michael › Pictures › Saved Pictures   ∨ ↺

5 The current folder address is highlighted

C:\Users\Michael\Pictures\Saved Pictures   ∨ ↺

6 Edit the folder address to the required location, for example C:\Users\Public\ Pictures, and then press Enter to go to that location

C:\Users\Public\Pictures   ∨ ↺

The Address bar displays the current location as a series of links, separated by arrows. There's an Up arrow at the left, to go up one level.

For common locations, you can type just the name; for example:
- Computer
- Contacts
- Control Panel
- Documents
- Pictures

Create Folders and Files

Hot tip

Create new folders to organize your documents by use or purpose, or create files of particular types, ready for use.

1 Open the library or folder where the new folder is required; for example, select This PC, Documents

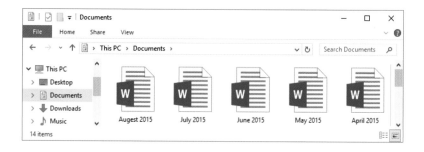

2 Right-click an empty part of the folder area and select New > Folder (or choose a particular file type)

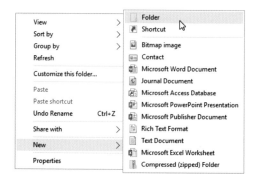

Don't forget

Choose one of the file types, for example a Microsoft PowerPoint presentation, and it will be initially named as New Microsoft PowerPoint Presentation. Overtype this name, as shown for the New folder in Step 3.

3 Overtype the name New folder with the required name, and press Enter (or click elsewhere)

If you create a folder or a file in a library, such as Documents or Pictures, it will be created and stored within the library's default save location; for example, the current user's My Documents or My Pictures.

Copy or Move Files

You can copy a file (or files) using the Windows clipboard:

1 Open the folder containing the file, right-click the file icon and select Copy (or press Ctrl + C)

Hot tip

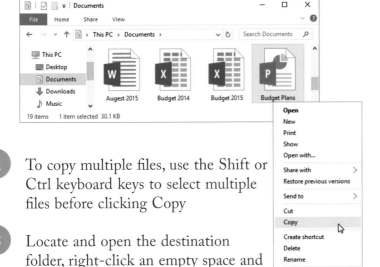

2 To copy multiple files, use the Shift or Ctrl keyboard keys to select multiple files before clicking Copy

3 Locate and open the destination folder, right-click an empty space and select Paste (or press Ctrl + V) to create a copy of the file in that folder

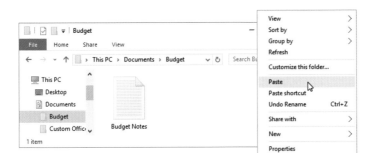

4 To move a file to a new location rather than make a copy, right-click the file icon and choose Cut (or press Ctrl + X)

5 The original file icon will be grayed out until you select Paste, when it will be moved to the new location

If your computer has a CD or DVD writer, Windows 10 allows you to write files onto blank CDs or DVDs. For example, to save files to disc as backups:

Insert your blank CD or DVD disc into the drive. From the Taskbar or Start menu, select File Explorer. Your blank disc will appear under Devices and drives. Double-click it.

When the Burn a Disc box appears, type a name for your disc in the "Disc title" field and choose With a CD/DVD player, then click Next. Copy and Paste (or drag and drop) the files and folders into the disc window.

Right-click a clear part of the window and select Burn to Disc. Select the desired recording speed (slower gives better quality). Click Next. When the disc is ready, remove it and store it safely.

...cont'd

To move or copy files using drag and drop operations:

1 Use File Explorer to locate and open the folder containing the files you want to move

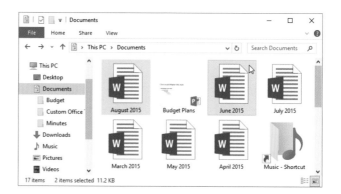

2 Select the first file then press the Ctrl key as you select the second and subsequent files

3 Click and hold any of the selected files, then drag the selection to the target folder and release there

4 To copy rather than move the files, | + Copy to Minutes | hold down Ctrl as you drag and release the selection

5 If the target folder is in a different drive, hold down Shift as you drag to move, otherwise you will copy

Delete Files

To remove files from a folder:

1 Select the file or files, and either right-click the selection and choose the Delete command, or press the keyboard Delete key

2 If the file is located anywhere other than your hard disk, you are asked to confirm permanent deletion

3 Files on the hard disk are moved to the Recycle Bin, usually with the warning message turned off

To recover a file deleted by mistake:

1 Right-click the Recycle Bin and select Open (or just double-click the icon)

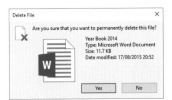

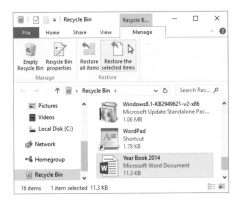

2 Select the file or files to be recovered and click Restore the selected items, on the Ribbon

3 The files are returned to their original locations

To turn on the warning message for hard disk files, right-click the Recycle Bin, then select Properties and tick Display delete confirmation dialog.

To remove hard disk files completely without using the Recycle Bin as an interim store, hold down Shift as you select Delete. You'll be asked to confirm. The deleted files then cannot be recovered.

Folder Views

File Explorer offers a variety of ways to view the files and sub-folders contained in folders and libraries:

1 Open a library or folder, for example Saved Pictures, and note the file list style in use (i.e. Large icons)

Hot tip

You can also change folder views using the File Explorer Ribbon (see pages 104-105), and selecting the View tab.

2 Right-click an empty part of the folder area and select View, to see the various styles, and the current setting marked with a bullet

3 Choose any of the four icon sizes to see the effects

Extra large icons

Large icons

Don't forget

The folders illustrated here have had their layouts changed to hide the Navigation and Details panes (see pages 106-107).

Medium icons

Small icons

For icon sizes other than Small, you can select Hide file names from the View menu.

...cont'd

Other views can offer more information about the files.

List

Details

A file-type icon rather than a thumbnail is used for Small icons, List and Details views.

Tiles

Content

The details provided with the Content view depend on the file type, and on the data provided when the file was created.

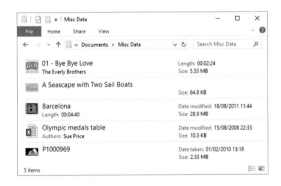

As with Views, you can also change Sort and Group attributes using the File Explorer Ribbon (see pages 104-105).

The options in the Sort by and Group by menus also depend on the type of file that the folder has been optimized for, i.e.:

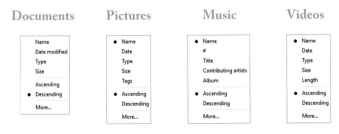

File Explorer Ribbon

You can also manage the appearance of libraries and folders using tabs and command groups on the File Explorer Ribbon.

The Ribbon is usually minimized, but it is expanded when you select Home, Share, View or Manage. You can also press the button next to Help (see page 97) to Expand, Pin or Minimize the ribbon.

1 Open File Explorer and, for example, select the Pictures library

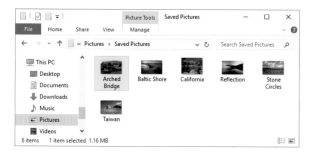

2 If there's no Ribbon, click a tab, e.g. the Home tab

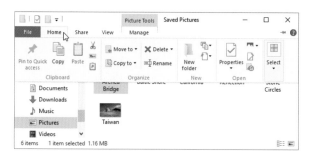

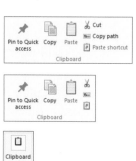

Where space permits, commands have icons with names. On narrower windows some become icons only, or get minimized to drop-down boxes.

3 To always show the Ribbon, right-click the tab bar and click Minimize the Ribbon, to uncheck the option

The Ribbon shows commands appropriate to the specific tab and grouped by function. Inactive commands are grayed out.

The Home Tab

The Home tab has commands for handling items in the folder.

...cont'd

The Share Tab
These commands are to help you make files and folders available to other users.

You can send files via email, write files to CD or DVD, and set up sharing across the network.

The View Tab
With these commands you can control the layout of folders and the appearance of items in the folders.

The Current view category includes Sort by and Group by, and Show/hide allows you to reveal hidden files.

The Manage Tabs
These are commands that are specific to the type of folder – Picture Tools and Library Tools, as shown.

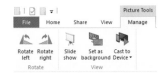 

The Manage tools displayed are based on the type of file for which the library or folder has been optimized.

The File Menu
Select File to open new windows, access Help and close File Explorer.

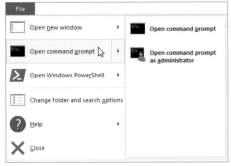

File Explorer Layout

You can control how libraries, folders and files are displayed in the File Explorer window. To illustrate the options:

1 Open File Explorer and, for example, select the Pictures library, and select the View tab

Don't forget

In this example, File Explorer shows the Ribbon, Navigation pane and Contents pane (with Large icons).

2 Click Preview pane on the Ribbon and choose the Details view, to choose the style of the Preview pane

Hot tip

In the Preview pane, you can see a preview or extended details of the selected file – useful when you use list views rather than graphical icons for the folder contents.

3 Click Details pane on the Ribbon and select List view, to choose the style of the Details pane

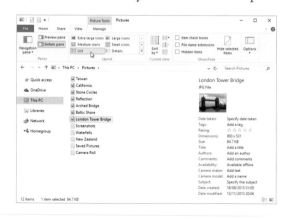

Don't forget

Preview pane and Details pane act as toggles – select one to switch off the other, or reselect the active pane to turn both off.

4 Click the Navigation pane button to display or hide Show all folders, libraries or the Navigation pane itself

Quick access has links to frequently accessed folders and recently opened files.

5 You can have the Navigation pane expand automatically to the currently-open folder

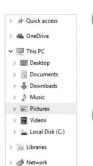

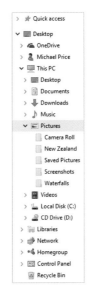

6 Show all folders puts the system folders, drives, libraries and network items in a hierarchical list starting at Desktop

When you are in a folder you access regularly, right-click Quick access and select Pin current folder to Quick access.

7 To change the pane sizes, resize the window. Move the mouse pointer over the line separator and drag with the resize arrow to change the ratios of each pane

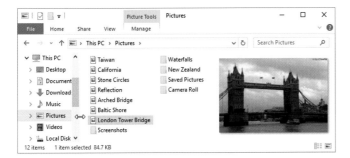

The preview shown depends on the file type. In the Documents folder, Word, WordPad or Notepad files can show text contents in the Preview pane. For other file types, you may see the message "No preview available".

The preview image is automatically resized to make full use of the Preview pane, while retaining the image proportions.

To display just the folder contents in the File Explorer windows (as shown in the image on page 100), uncheck all of the Navigation pane options and deselect the Preview pane and the Details option.

Search Box

If you want to access a file, but are not sure which sub-folder it is in, you can start at the higher-level folder and use the Search box to find the exact location.

1 Open, for example, the Music library in File Explorer

The search looks for matches with file names, file types, text content, file tags and other file properties.

You don't have to worry about using capital letters. Use quotation marks to match to a phrase rather than individual words.

2 Click the Search box and start typing the search words; e.g. love is all around

3 As you type, matches so far are listed

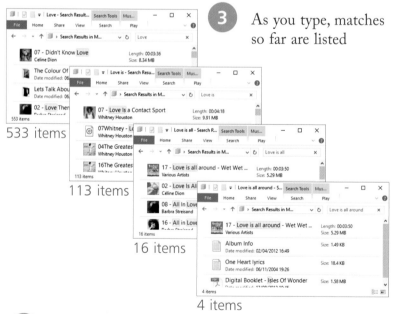

533 items

113 items

16 items

4 items

You can also find files and folders using Cortana, the Personal Digital Assistant.

Don't forget

At any stage, you can select the required file from the list of results and double-click to open or run it.

4 Stop typing when the results show the file you are seeking or when you have completed your search request

In the example, the results include a song of that title, related album information and the song lyrics.

6 Classic Applications

Windows 10 includes some useful Classic applications for calculating, text editing, word processing and picture editing, and you can search the internet for external programs to handle other functions.

Classic Applications

Windows 10 provides the operating environment for a variety of applications. In many cases, these are supplied as separate programs or a suite of programs. However, some of the desired functions may be in the form of small but potentially very useful programs included with Windows under Windows Accessories. The main application areas and the included Windows programs are:

- Text processing –   Sticky Notes, Notepad
- Word processing –   WordPad
- Electronic mail –   Windows Fax and Scan
- Drawing –   Paint
- Spreadsheet –   Math Input Panel
- Database –   Character Map, Steps Recorder
- Multimedia –   Snipping Tool, XPS Viewer

Don't forget

These applications take advantage of Windows 10 features and can be pinned as tiles on the Start menu, but they do not operate as Universal apps (see page 38).

You'll find these listed in All Apps, on the Start menu.

Windows 10 also offers a large selection of system and administrative tools.

Some apps, e.g. Windows Media Player and XPS Viewer, aren't installed on every system. Select Settings, Apps, Apps & Features, and click Manage optional features. Then add any apps you desire.

Don't forget

Some programs that were previously supplied as Windows Accessories are being provided as Universal apps; e.g. Calculator, and Microsoft Edge (taking the place of Internet Explorer).

For functions that are not provided by the programs included with Windows, you'll need to install separate programs or a suite of programs such as Adobe Acrobat or Microsoft Office. If you don't want to install the full applications, you can download free readers and viewers, to display the files and documents that those applications create.

Notepad

Notepad is a text editor that you can use to create, view or modify text (.txt) files. It provides only very basic formatting, and handles text, a line at a time.

1 Search for Notepad in the Taskbar Search box, or select it from the Windows Accessories folder in the All Apps list; open the program, then type some text, pressing Enter for each new line

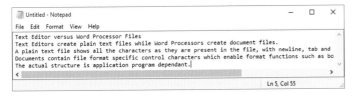

2 Select File, Save As, and type the required file name (with file type .txt) then click Save

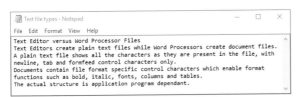

3 If the text is longer than the window, select Format and click Word Wrap, to fit the text lines within the window size

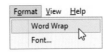

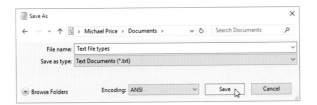

4 When you print the file, it will wrap according to the paper width, regardless of the word-wrap setting

WordPad

WordPad also offers text editing, but adds tools and facilities for more complex formatting of individual pieces of text.

WordPad uses the Ribbon rather than a Menu bar. There are two tabs: Home and View. The File button provides Save, Setup and Print functions.

1 Start WordPad from Windows Accessories in the All Apps list, and enter text, pressing Enter for each new paragraph

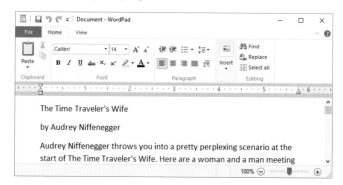

Click the left, center or right alignment buttons to adjust the positioning of the selected paragraph or line of text.

2 Use the formatting bar to change the font, size, style and color for selected (highlighted) text

Save WordPad documents as .rtf (Rich Text Format) to retain the text formatting. Saving as .txt will remove the formatting (and images or links).

3 Click the Save button on the Quick access toolbar (or press Ctrl + S) to save the document

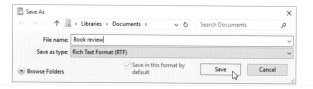

Insert Pictures

WordPad also allows you to include pictures in documents.

1 Position the typing cursor and click Insert then the Picture button on the Home tab

2 Locate and select the picture, then click Open

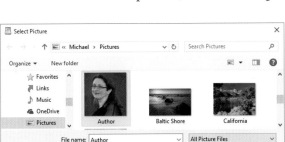

Hot tip

You can also click the Paint drawing button, to insert a drawing that you create using Paint (see pages 114-115).

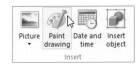

3 A copy of the image is added to the document and displayed at the cursor location

Don't forget

WordPad can open text files in a variety of formats, including Open XML, Unicode Text and Microsoft Office .docx (but not the older .doc format).

Rich Text Format (*.rtf)
Office Open XML Document (*.docx)
OpenDocument Text (*.odt)
Text Documents (*.txt)
Text Documents - MS-DOS Format (*.txt)
Unicode Text Documents (*.txt)
All Wordpad Documents (*.rtf, *.docx, *.odt, *.txt)
All Documents (*.*)

4 If it's the wrong size, right-click the picture, select Resize picture and choose the scale factor required

Paint

Paint is a digital sketchpad that can be used to draw, color and edit pictures. These can be images that you create from scratch, or you can modify existing pictures, such as digital photographs or web page graphics. For example:

1 Select Paint from Windows Accessories in the All Apps list, or from the Start menu, to start up with a blank canvas

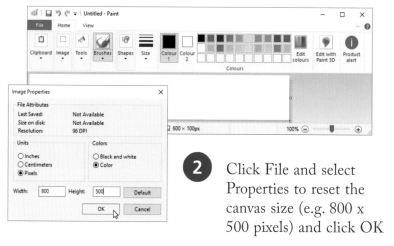

2 Click File and select Properties to reset the canvas size (e.g. 800 x 500 pixels) and click OK

3 Select the arrow below Paste, select Paste from, locate the picture to add to the canvas, and click Open

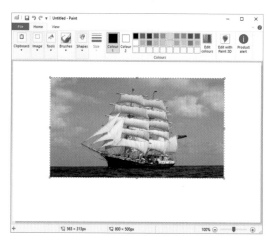

4 Drag the image to position it centrally, with space for a title

5 Click Shapes, select the Rounded Rectangle tool, then click and drag to draw a frame around the picture

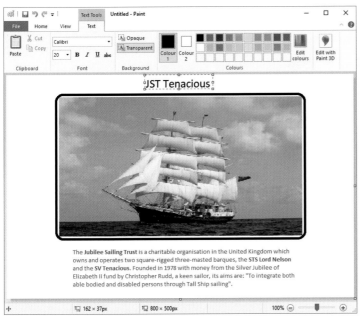

6 Use the Text tool to draw a text box and add information such as a description of the contents

7 To make changes, select the View tab and click the Zoom in button, or the Magnifier

8 When you've finished making changes, select File, Save, type the file name and click Save

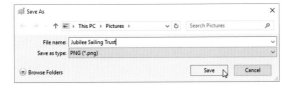

Unknown File Types

Windows and its applications cannot help when you receive attachments or download files of unknown file types, but it will do its best to search for alternative options.

1 If there are unknown file types in your current folder, the extensions (normally hidden) are displayed

You can also right-click the file and select Open with, to get the initial suggestions.

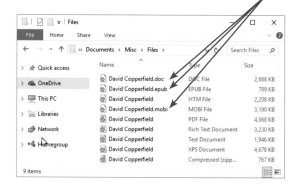

2 Double-click an unknown type, e.g. the DOC file, and you're asked how you want to open it

Beware

If there's nothing appropriate, just press the Esc key. Anything you do choose gets remembered, if you select the Always use this app... box, even if it doesn't work for that file type.

3 Click More apps to view the suggested programs. If none are suitable, select Look for an app in the (Windows) Store and click OK

116

Hot tip

If the Store does not find a good answer, you can search the internet for software, as shown on the following page.

4 There may be many apps offered, some free and some chargeable, so you'll have to pick out the one you think most suitable

Search the Web for Software

If there's no obvious choice from the Windows suggestions, you can search the internet for suitable software.

1 To get information about the use and purpose of an unknown file type, visit **FilExt** at **http://filext.com**

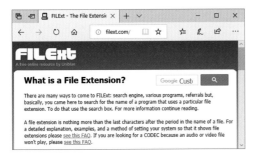

FilExt is a free online service by UniBlue, the PC Tools supplier. They, of course, take the opportunity to remind you about their products.

2 For a DOC file extension, select letter D from the index and scroll down to locate entries for .DOC

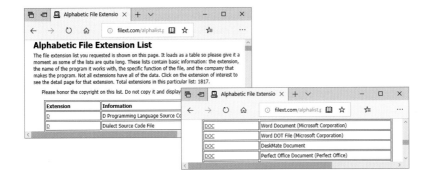

The .DOC extension has been used by many programs over the years. Microsoft Word is the most likely entry in this case.

.DOC File
File extension: DOC
File type: Document

3 Select the most appropriate entry; e.g. Word Document (Microsoft Corporation)

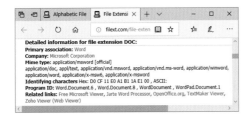

...cont'd

Beware

There may be a link for a free Microsoft Viewer, but Microsoft has now withdrawn the Word Viewer product.

4 To view Word documents without Microsoft Office, select one of the suggested links; e.g. TextMaker Viewer

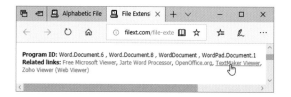

5 Click the title link and follow the instructions to download the setup program and then run it

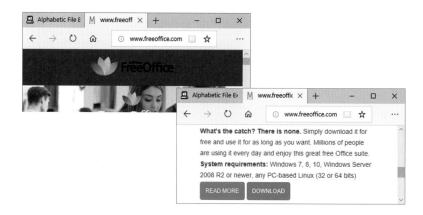

Don't forget

An entry for SoftMaker FreeOffice 2018 is added to the All Apps list (but by default it is not pinned to the Start menu).

6 When prompted, register as a user and install Free Office

7 When installation completes, the .DOC files are recognized and will open in Word Viewer

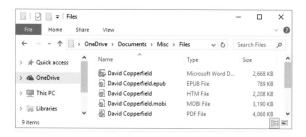

Change Default Program

With FreeOffice installed, you now have several programs that can load Rich Text Format documents. To review the options and confirm the default program for .rtf files:

1 Right-click any .rtf file and select Open with... to list the programs available on your system

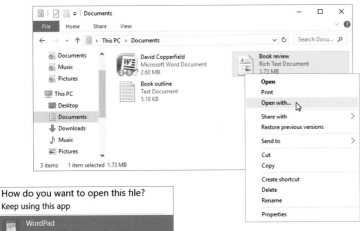

2 WordPad (the default) and the FreeOffice programs are both shown

3 To change the default, select an alternative, click the Always use this app to open box, then click OK

4 The icons for the files indicate that the .rtf file uses WordPad as default, the .doc file uses FreeOffice TextMaker, while the .txt file uses Notepad

Hot tip

You can review and change the default program that is associated with any particular file type.

Hot tip

To open a file with a different program, without changing the default, choose the program and make sure the box is clear before clicking OK.

Don't forget

If you have Microsoft Office installed, it can open all three file types and may set itself as the default.

Tablet Mode

The examples shown previously have all featured Windows apps running in the Desktop mode. They will also operate in Tablet mode, but each program runs full-screen.

1 Start WordPad and Paint, and switch between them with Alt + Tab, or using the Task View button

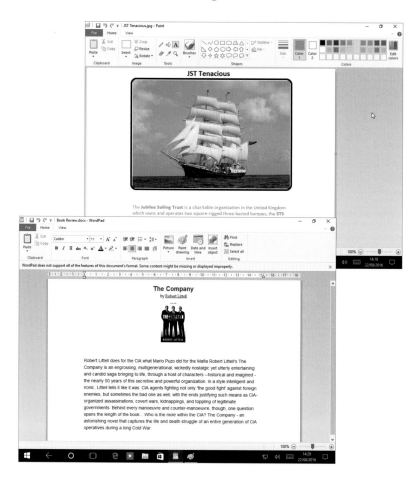

There are Title bars, with Minimize, Maximize/Restore and Close buttons, but the Maximize/Restore buttons do not function, and the windows cannot be resized.

The Snap Assist function is supported, so the screen can be split to run two apps side by side, each using half of the screen. However, the four-app split (see page 41) is not supported in Tablet mode.

7 Universal Apps

The emphasis is now on Universal apps in Windows 10. Some, such as Reader and OneDrive, are supplied at installation. However, there are many Universal apps at the Microsoft Store, where you can search, review descriptions, then download and install apps on your system.

Sources for Apps

Although Windows Classic applications are supported, the main functions are provided by Universal apps in Windows 10. As already discussed, these can run full-screen or windowed, and can use Windows Snap Assist to allow two or more apps to share the screen.

The primary design point for the Universal app is the touchscreen as exemplified by the tablet PC, but all the apps can also be operated on a system with standard monitor, mouse and keyboard equipment.

The Windows apps that are available can be found in just two places:

1 Supplied and installed with Windows 10

This is a typical Start menu for a newly-installed Windows 10 system, showing some of the Windows apps you may expect to find installed.

2 Via download and install from the Microsoft Store

The range of Universal apps available at the Microsoft Store changes frequently, as new products are added and others are removed or revised.

Programs submitted to Microsoft can also include Classic apps. These are conventional applications that are listed in the Microsoft Store, but provided from the manufacturer's website via a link that is included with the application description. These, and other conventional apps, may still be obtained directly, without visiting the Microsoft Store.

In the past, Windows applications have been available from many sources, including supplier and enthusiast websites, as well as Microsoft. Sources for Windows apps are now much more limited.

All Universal apps must be submitted to Microsoft for certification before they are allowed in the Microsoft Store (or included on installation discs).

Supplied with Windows 10

The details may change with updates to Windows 10, or with customization by your computer supplier, but these are the Universal apps that were initially included on the installation disc, or added during initial setup.

To see all of the apps on your system, switch to the Start menu and scroll the All Apps list.

There are more than 40 Universal apps shown on this example of an All Apps list. Your list may also feature apps that are Most used or Recently added. By default, about 20 of the apps have tiles on the Start menu. Those that are not shown there can always be pinned to Start if desired.

Use the full-screen Start menu, or the All Apps button in Tablet mode, to display the list of apps.

There are four different sizes of tile, and you can select the size you prefer for each individual app. The Large and Wide options are particularly suitable for Live tiles that display real-time information. However, not all apps support the Large option and some apps are restricted to the Medium and Small options. To change the size:

 1 Right-click the tile and select Resize, and select from the options offered for that app

On the following pages we will look at the Calculator, Alarms & Clock and other apps. Other apps, such as Mail, Microsoft Edge, Music and Photos, will be discussed in the relevant chapters on the specific topics.

You can also pin Windows Accessories and other conventional Windows apps as tiles on the Start menu.

Calculator

While it is no substitute for a full spreadsheet application, the Windows Calculator app provides quite powerful computational facilities.

1 Select Calculator from the All Apps list on the Start menu

2 In Standard mode, type or click to enter the calculation using the desired operation symbol, and press = to display the result

Click the function buttons or press the equivalent keyboard keys, to perform Add, Subtract, Multiply, Divide, Square Root, Percentage and Inverse operations. You can also store and recall numbers from memory, and the History capability keeps track of stages in the calculations.

In addition to the Standard mode, there are also Scientific and Programmer modes, plus a variety of Converter options provided:

1 Open Calculator, then click the Menu button to list the modes

2 Select Scientific to see the features

Scientific mode offers a variety of logarithmic, trigonometric and factorial functions in various forms, such as Degrees, Radians, etc.

Don't forget

You can also use the numeric keypad on your keyboard to type numbers and operators. Press Num Lock if it is not already turned on.

124

Don't forget

You'll also find a large number of equivalent apps at the Microsoft Store if you search for Calculator.

3 Select Programmer mode just to see what it offers

The Programmer calculator operates in decimal, hexadecimal, octal and binary. It supports byte, word, dword and qword. There's a full keypad, including alphabetics for hex numbers, and an alternative bit-toggling keypad.

Unlike the other Calculator modes, Programmer mode does not maintain a history of computations.

There are 12 different Converter options, each with a range of units.

4 Select the Converter mode, and select a category, for example Weight and Mass, and choose the From and To units; e.g. Kilograms to Pounds

Note how the Converter suggests equivalents, using other units including (in this example) number of footballs.

Each of the categories offers a range of appropriate units, and they all suggest equivalents to your results, sometimes quite idiosyncratic in nature:

Weight and Mass has a total of 14 units that you can convert between.

5 Switch to the Energy category to convert between Food calories and Kilojoules

6 Enter 2500 as the starting value

You are told that this is about equal to 9914 BTUs or 9.99 slices of cake!

Alarms & Clock

This app is a combination of an Alarm Clock, World Clock, Timer and a Stopwatch. You can use it to set alarms and reminders, to check the time anywhere in the world, and to time activities.

1 Select Alarms & Clock from the All Apps list (or search for it via the Search box)

2 Select each of the four types of clock in turn to review the features that are offered

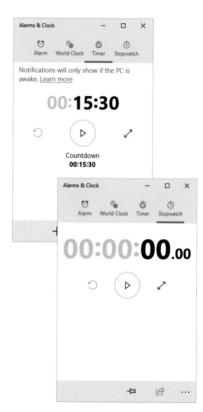

3 Click the New (+) button to add a new item, click the Select button to remove items, and click See more (...) to show additional commands

Weather

This app displays forecasts of temperature, wind direction and speed, humidity etc., for your default or chosen location.

1 Select the Weather tile from the Start menu to see the overview by day

2 Scroll down to see the details for the selected day

The Weather app runs on other devices such as tablets and smartphones, and adjusts itself to suit their particular screen sizes.

Select a specific day, and view the Hourly Forecast, Summary or Details as desired.

Click the buttons on the Icon bar to display Maps, Historical Weather, Places or News. Click the Menu button to show categories for the app.

Microsoft Store

The Microsoft Store recognizes which version of Windows your system is running and displays apps appropriate for you. To see what's offered:

1 Touch or click the Microsoft Store tile on the Start menu or the Microsoft Store icon on the Taskbar to open the Home page for the Store

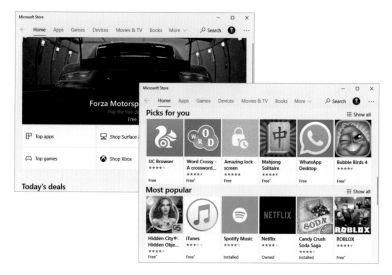

2 You'll see highlighted apps and Top apps; Featured; Top games; Collections; and other groupings

3 Scroll down to see some Picks for you, and click Show all to see the full set of apps being suggested

Don't forget

You can also scroll down the Home page to see sets including:
- Most popular
- Top free apps
- Top free games
- New music
- New movies
- Top-selling TV shows
- Collections

Each displays a subset of items, with a Show all link to the full set.

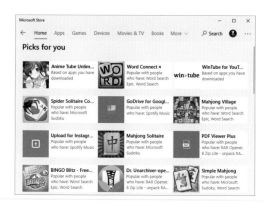

App Categories

To see what categories of apps are offered:

1 Select the Apps page and scroll to the bottom

2 Review the list of 25 categories of apps provided

3 Click a group, e.g. Utilities & tools, to display the Top free apps available in that category

The entry for each app shows if it is already installed, or available for download free of charge, or at a price.

The price stated will be in the currency appropriate to your location; e.g. Dollars for the USA, and Sterling for the UK.

Hot tip

The Microsoft Store for Windows 10 systems is arranged in various groupings, to help you explore its contents and find apps that are useful to you.

Don't forget

Select an alternative grouping, for example Best-rated or Trending, to view the apps of that type.

Books & Reference

You can use categories to explore the Microsoft Store's contents:

1 Select a category of interest, for example Books & reference

Each app in the Store is assigned to a specific category and subcategory. For Books & reference, the subcategories are:

E-reader
Fiction
Nonfiction
Reference

You can use the subcategories included in Store descriptions as search terms to help locate relevant apps.

2 Scroll down the screen to see more Top free apps

3 Select another filter such as Best selling, to show apps of that type in the selected category

Note that any apps you have installed on another system (using the same Microsoft Account), but not on the current system, will be shown as Owned. When you select such an app to view details, it will be shown as ready to install on the current machine.

Search Microsoft Store

You can use the Search button found on every Microsoft Store screen to view its scope and find items of interest.

1 Select the Search button and type a search term; e.g. books

2 The top few matches are displayed immediately

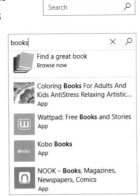

3 Click the magnifying glass icon to show all the results

The app you want may not always be classified under the category you'd expect, so it is always useful to search the whole Store using your terms of interest.

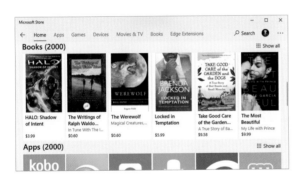

You'll find varied results in multiple categories, such as Games, Movies and TV shows, as well as in Apps.

4 Select the App group to refine the listing and show only the available apps

Books (2000)
Apps (2000)
Games (58)
Movies (57)
TV shows (42)
Hardware (1)

You can further refine the search results by selecting one of the 25 categories of app, or by adding an appropriate subcategory as a search term.

Installing Apps

Don't forget

If you already own this app, you'll see the Install button (or Launch button, if already installed) rather than the Get button.

Hot tip

During the process, messages from the Microsoft Store let you know the progress of the actions being performed.

1 Find an app you want to investigate; for example Freda epub reader

2 If you decide you want this app on your system, click the Get button

3 When the app downloads and installs, Launch it directly from the Microsoft Store entry

4 You'll also find entries for the app in Recently added, and on the All Apps list

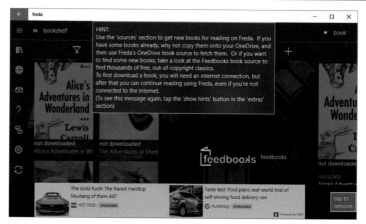

5 Right-click either entry in All Apps and select Pin to Start to add a tile to the Start menu

Your App Account

From the Microsoft Store, you can check your account and see what apps you have installed, even if you use your Microsoft Account on multiple machines.

1. Open the Store app and click See more (...), then select View account from the drop-down menu displayed

2. Microsoft Edge opens the web page for your Microsoft Account

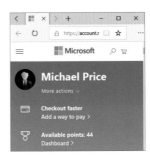

3. Your account is displayed with details of your recent purchases from the Microsoft Store

Don't forget

Purchases include free apps as well as those you've paid for.

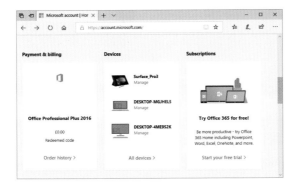

4. Scroll down to see more details about your Microsoft Account

Beware

You can install apps from the Store, free or charged, on up to ten Windows 10 devices, including PCs, tablets, smartphones and gaming devices, all associated with the same Microsoft Account, although you are limited to four devices for Music and Video apps.

Your Library

Click Show all to see all apps or games you have installed on any device using your Microsoft Account, as long as they are compatible with your current system (even if installed under an earlier Windows version).

1 From the Microsoft Store app, click See more (...) and select My Library

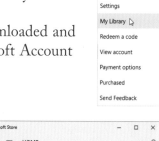

2 The recent apps you've downloaded and installed using your Microsoft Account will be listed

3 Scroll down to see your recent games

4 Select an entry to see its status on the current device

If you already own an app or a game, but it's not installed on the current device, you'll see a Download button alongside its Library entry. This is not visible when the item is installed.

5 You can click the Download button to install an app or game on the current device

134

Updates

If any Universal app that you've installed gets updated, the changes are supplied through the Microsoft Store. In Windows 10, these updates are applied automatically in the background, without any notification by default.

If you'd prefer to manually accept and install updates:

1 Select Settings from See more (...) drop-down menu in the Microsoft Store

2 Drag the button marked Update apps automatically to Off, to reverse the action and turn off updates

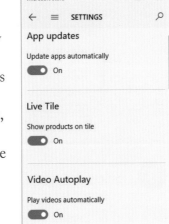

3 To view the Update status, select Downloads and updates from the See more (...) drop-down menu in the Microsoft Store

4 The available updates are listed and can be individually downloaded, or you can select Update all

5 Drag the button back to On again, to restore the automatic updating

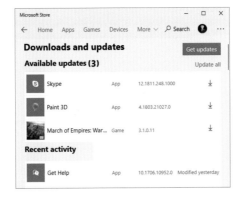

Beware

This option is not available on Windows 10 Home edition, so app updates will always be applied automatically.

Don't forget

When you drag a button on or off, it will change color from the Accent color (On) to White (Off) or vice versa, to indicate the new status.

Verify Identity

For some actions within Windows 10, you may be asked to verify your identity with a security code. For example:

You can select either an email address or a telephone number, depending what contact information is in the profile for your Microsoft Account.

1 Sign on to your PC with a Local account, and open the Microsoft Store. Click the User icon (no user image shown) and select Sign in

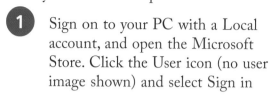

2 Follow the prompts to Sign in to your Microsoft Account with your user name and password

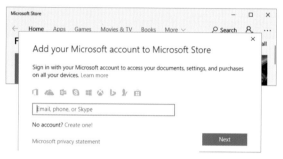

3 Select how you'd like to get the code, and click Next

When you've signed in and had your account verified, you'll see a User image on the User icon.

4 Enter the code that you receive and click Next. Your account will then be verified by Microsoft and you will be able to continue with the desired action

Authenticator App

1 Visit the app store for your mobile device; an iPad for example

2 Search the app store for "microsoft authenticator"

You can use an app on your mobile device instead, so you can receive security codes at any time and any place, even if there's no phone service (see page 138).

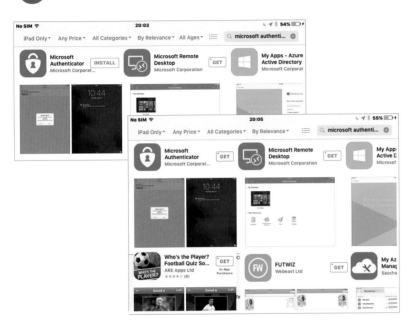

3 Select Get and then select Install for the Microsoft Authenticator app, to add it to your mobile device

This illustrates adding the Microsoft Authenticator app for the iPad. A similar process will be needed to add the equivalent app for your smartphone.

...cont'd

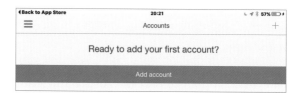

The app is now ready for you to add the Microsoft Accounts you may need to verify:

You can be added as a new user to any Windows 10 device, and use your Microsoft Account to sign in to that device.

1 Click Add account and specify the type; e.g. Personal account

2 Follow prompts to sign in to the Microsoft Account and validate it one last time with a code, and the account is added to the app

Don't forget

If your device containing the Authenticator app is not to hand, you can still use the email or phone methods for verifying your identity.

3 The next time you need to verify your identity, it will call upon the Microsoft Authenticator, and you can approve the request on your mobile device

8 Email and Calendar

Windows 10 provides the Mail app for email communications, the People app to manage your contacts, and the Calendar app to keep track of events and meetings. Communicate instantly using the Skype app. For email and time management you can also use Outlook from Office 2016.

Electronic Mail

Email or electronic mail is used to send and receive digital messages. You can send an email message to anyone with an email address, you can receive messages from anyone who knows your email address, and you can reply to those messages or forward them to another email address. You can send your email message to more than one person at the same time and attach files such as documents or pictures.

Email is free, since no stamp or fee is required. However, before you can use email, you require:

- An account with an Internet Service Provider (ISP).

- An internet connection such as telephone or cable.

- A modem or router to make the connection.

- An email address from your email service provider or from a web service such as Gmail or Hotmail.

- An email program such as Mail or Outlook 2016.

An email address consists of a username or nickname, the @ sign, and the server name of your email provider, e.g. jsmith99@myisp.com or web service, e.g. jsmith99@gmail.com

Mail
This is the Windows app that is installed along with Calendar and People, when Windows 10 is set up. It provides full-screen access to multiple email accounts.

Outlook 2016
This application is included in all editions of Microsoft Office 2016 except the Home & Student edition, and is installed with Windows 10 systems that have Office 2016 added. It provides fully functioning email and time management services, and runs on the Desktop as a windowed application (see pages 155-156).

Other Email Programs
There are many other apps in the Microsoft Store that supplement the features of the Mail app. For example, Email Backgrounds provides colorful email stationery.

You can access instant messaging (and make video and phone calls) using the Skype app pre-installed in Windows 10. Select Skype (see page 152) to get started.

Windows 10 Mail App

To get started with the Mail app:

1 On the Start menu select the tile for the Mail app

2 The Mail app is launched

To add another email account when there are existing accounts, click Add account, otherwise click Go to inbox.

3 Mail identifies your Microsoft Account as Outlook.com, ready for you to select

4 Mail shows any accounts you may have already added. If there's no existing email account, Mail automatically invokes Add account

5 Select your account type, for example Yahoo Mail, enter your email address and then click Next

141

You may need to give permission for the Mail and Calendar to access the email account messages, contacts and calendar data.

6 Enter the password for your email account and then click Next

7 Click Done when the account has been added successfully

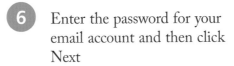

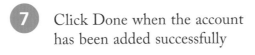

...cont'd

If you have multiple email accounts, click the Accounts icon to change accounts.

Click the Expand/ Collapse button on the icon bar to display the titles for the icons, and list Accounts and Folders.

When Mail starts up, the display layout that you see depends on the screen resolution. On a higher resolution monitor, in this case 1280 x 1024 pixels, you'll see three panes – Expanded Icon bar, Current Folder and Reading.

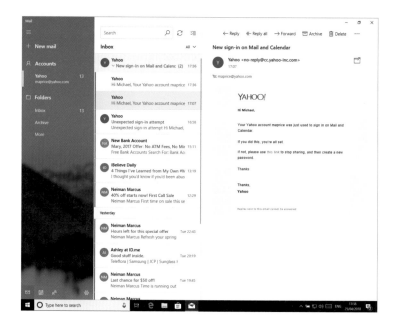

On a lower resolution monitor (the example below is just 1024 x 768 pixels) you'll see only two folders, the Current Folder and Reading panes, plus the Icon bar.

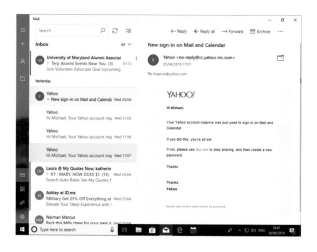

Mail App Settings

1 Click Settings on the Icon bar to show all the options

2 Select Manage Accounts to choose an account and edit its settings

3 Click Add account if you want to define another email account to use with the Mail app

4 Select Personalization to select an image for the Reading pane, displayed when no message is selected

5 Select Signature to specify a default email signature to be appended to the messages you send from a specific account, or from all accounts

Don't forget

Quick Action icons for Archive, Delete and Flag icons are displayed when you move the mouse pointer over a message in the Inbox.

6 Select Notifications to customize the notification settings, again for a specific account or for all of your accounts

7 Select other entries in the Settings list to see which of them apply to your particular system

The Mail Window

These are the main elements of the Mail window:

Accounts

Selected Account

Selected Message

Selected Folder

Folder List

Settings

Mail, Calendar and People

Mailbox Folder

Reading Pane

Respond

Delete

More Options

Folder (Inbox) Pane

Message Contents

Hot tip

The Mail tile on the Start menu displays the message count and message extracts (even if Mail is closed). The message count may also appear on the Taskbar icon.

1 Click More Options (...) at the top right of the window to display commands for dealing with the messages in your Mailbox

2 Click the Zoom button to list the scale factors offered

3 Click the arrow at the top of the Zoom list to return to the Options list. Click anywhere on the Mail window away from the lists to remove them

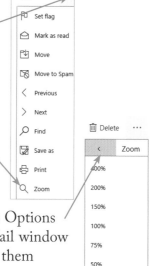

View Messages

1 Select a message from the Folder pane and it displays in the Reading pane

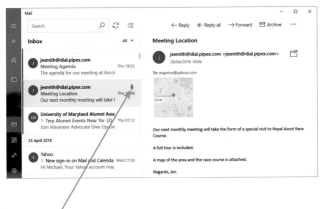

Pictures can be included in the body of email messages, as well as saved from them. Other files such as documents can also be sent, saved or opened from a message.

2 If there is an attachment (as indicated by a paperclip icon) it will be contained within the email body or shown as a link

3 Click Reply to respond to the sender, Reply all for all addressees, or Forward to send to another person

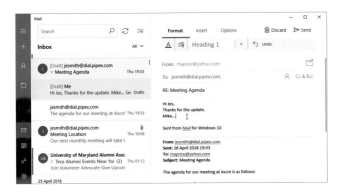

You can add recipients from your Contacts list (see pages 148-149).

4 Type your reply and click the Send button when finished

5 A copy is saved in the Sent folder of the account used to send the reply

People

Windows 10 allows you to collect details of all your contacts and make them available to apps such as Mail and Calendar, via the People app.

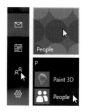

Don't forget

The People app can manage all contacts associated with your email and personal networking, but you need to define which accounts to use.

1 Click the People entry on the All Apps list (or its tile on the Start menu)

2 Click the Settings icon to display Settings with its list of linked accounts

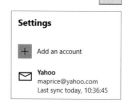

3 To start with, there may be just your Microsoft Account, with its associated contacts

Settings

➕ Add an account

✉ Yahoo
maprice@yahoo.com
Last sync today, 10:36:45

Hot tip

The accounts that you add will be included in the list displayed by Settings.

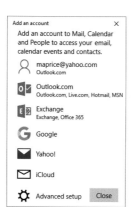

4 To define another account, click Add an account

5 Windows 10 will identify the types of account that have contacts that you may want to make available

6 Follow the prompts to set up the account and add the contacts to the Mail, Calendar and People apps

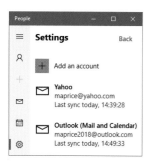

Managing Contacts

1 Click the Settings icon to show the Settings for People

2 Choose your preferred sort sequence, and how you'd like names to be displayed

3 Select Filter contact list and you can choose to Hide contacts without phone numbers

4 You can also choose the accounts to show contacts from, to manage the size of the list

5 To work with a specific contact, click that entry

6 Select Edit to make changes to the details for the contact, selecting which account to change if needed

Settings	Back
Contact list display	

Automatically add contacts that you have communicated with recently

On

Sort contact list by

● First Name
○ Surname

Display names by

● First name Surname
○ Surname, First name

Settings
Filter contact list
Pick which accounts you'll see

Filter contacts
Hide contacts without phone numbers
Off
Shows only the contacts that you can call or text. You can still find the rest by searching.

Show contacts from
☑ Microsoft account
☑ Skype
☐ Recent contacts for maprice@yahoo.com (Microsoft People)
☑ Yahoo
☑ Outlook (Mail and Calendar)

Done   Cancel

Click the New button on the People app Icon bar and you can enter the details for a new contact.

Details for contacts include name, phone numbers and email IDs and addresses (home, work and other). You can also add Other fields such as Website and Birthday.

Website
Significant other
Children
Birthday
Anniversary
Notes

+ Other

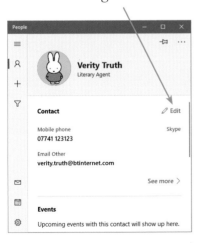

7 Select the Save button to record the changes that you've made

147

Create a Message

Hot tip

You can select a contact in People and double-click the email address to open Mail. You'll be asked to pick which account to send the message from.

Don't forget

When entering contact names in the To: box, you may see several suggestions that match so far, but the number reduces as you enter more of the name.

1 In Mail, select the email account, go to the Inbox and click the New mail button (or press Ctrl + N)

2 A blank message is displayed, ready for recipient details and content

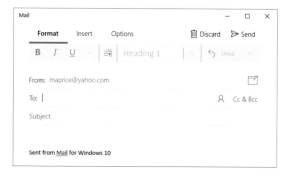

3 Begin typing the contact name in the To: box, then select the contact when it appears in the results below

4 Add more recipients in the same way, selecting from the suggestions where appropriate. Entries will be separated by semi-colons

5 Click in the Subject box and type the text for the title of the message

6 Click in the body of the message and add the salutation and the message text

7 End with your name, then the email signature for the sending account will be added automatically, if you have this set up (see Step 11 on the next page)

...cont'd

8 Select Cc & Bcc to add boxes for recipients who will be copied on the email

9 You can format the text in your message if you wish – click the Styles button to see more options

10 There are also Font formatting and Paragraph formatting options

11 To see your email signature, display the Mail Settings (see page 143), click Options and select the sending account

(see page 143)

12 Click the Send button to send the message

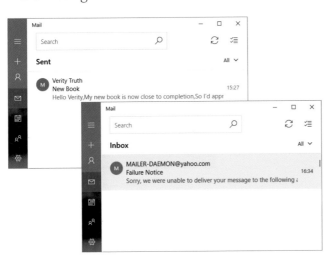

A copy of the message is kept in the Sent folder of the sending account. Should there be any problems with the email addresses used for the recipients, you may receive a message from the Mail Delivery System describing the problem and its cause.

Hot tip

Recipients added using Bcc (Blind carbon-copy) will not be shown on the copies of the message that others receive.

Don't forget

Note that any changes to the signature text will not affect the current message but will apply to future messages only.

Don't forget

Sometimes a message to an email address may fail, perhaps because the domain server is offline for a period. After several attempts, an error response message may be returned to you.

Calendar

Don't forget

You can use the icons on the bottom left-hand panel or the Icon bar, to switch between Mail and Calendar.

Hot tip

The first time you run Calendar, it lists the accounts (linked via Mail and People) and offers their associated calendars.

Hot tip

Click the down-arrow next to a calendar group to select from all the calendars associated with your accounts.

1 Click the Start menu and select the Calendar app tile (or All Apps entry)

2 You may be asked to let Mail and Calendar access your location. This enables Mail and Calendar to select appropriate public holidays and show local weather

3 Calendar opens, usually in the default Month view

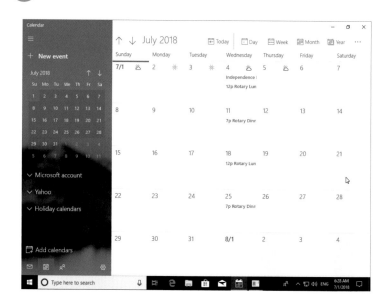

4 Click a day to add an event; either timed or All day

5 Enter the event name and tick All day, or choose start and end times, add the location and any other details, then click Done

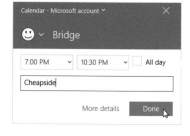

6 Click the Expand/Collapse button to replace the left-hand calendar panel with an Icon bar (see previous page)

(see previous page)

You can scroll Month view vertically, a month at a time, up and down, using the arrow buttons.

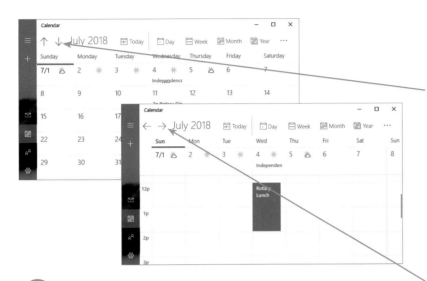

You can scroll Week views horizontally, seven days at a time, using the left and right arrow buttons. Use the scroll bar to move vertically through the hours.

151

7 In the top menu bar, select Week to display seven days at a time (or select Work week from the drop-down menu on Week to display five days, excluding the weekend)

8 Select Day view to see a single day's events

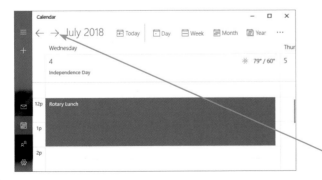

You can scroll Day view horizontally, a day at a time, using the left and right arrow buttons. Use the scroll bar to move vertically through the hours.

9 In any of the views, press the Today button to return focus to the current date

Skype to Stay in Touch

The Skype app offers free video and telephone call facilities, as well as being ideal for instant messaging. It is a Universal app and is included by default in Windows 10. To set Skype up, ready to use:

1 Select Skype from the All Apps list

2 Alternatively, select the Skype app tile on the Start menu

3 The first time you launch Skype it asks you several questions about the level of access you wish to allow

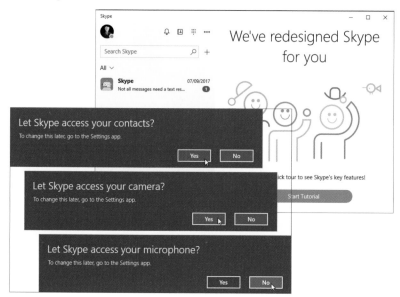

Don't forget

The Tutorial explains the use of the New, Profile, Call and Contacts icons displayed at the top of the screen.

4 Respond Yes or No as appropriate for each question

5 Click the Start Tutorial button to display a brief overview of Skype

6 Experiment with the options, using your Microsoft account as a Skype ID, or Sign out if you want to use a different Skype ID

7 Next time you start Skype, you can Sign in with your existing account or with a different account

You may get a number of suggestions of Skype users that may match. Ensure that you have chosen the correct one before communicating.

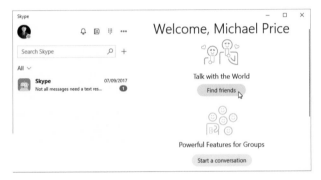

8 Find friends, or Start a conversation with a group

9 To change Skype appearance, select More (...), Settings, and choose Light or Dark or stay with the Windows default

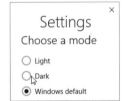

Your new mode will be applied immediately – no need to close and then restart Skype.

Windows 10 and Office

Windows 10 systems do not normally include Microsoft Office as an installed option, unless it gets added as an extra by the system supplier. However, there are several ways you can find facilities to help you work with Office documents.

1 Go to **products.office.com/en-us/office-online** to get free use of Office applications via your browser

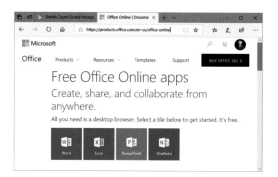

2 If you have a tablet or phone system, you can search Microsoft Store to find free mobile versions of PowerPoint, Excel and Word

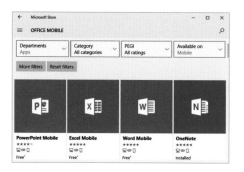

3 For the full versions of the Office applications, go to **products.office. com/en-us/try** for a free one-month trial of Office 365, or to take out a subscription to the product

Outlook 2016

With Office 365 or Office 2016 (all editions except Home & Student) installed on your Windows 10 system, you'll have Outlook 2016 as an alternative for email messages and time management.

1 Select the entry for Outlook 2016 in the All Apps list (labeled as Outlook)

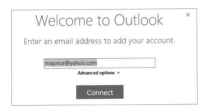

2 Accept the suggested account or type another email account, then click Connect

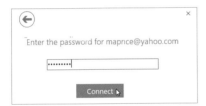

3 Specify the password for the chosen account, then click Connect to continue

4 Connection to the account is automatically established and account setup is completed. Clear the check box if you don't want Outlook on your phone (see page 156 if you do want this), then click OK

The Microsoft Office 2016 applications may have been pinned to the Start menu on your system, and from here you can then select the Outlook 2016 tile.

If Outlook cannot automatically connect to your email account, select Advanced options and tick the box to Let me set up my account manually. Then select the account type and provide server details, security settings etc.

...cont'd

Hot tip

On the Ribbon, select View, Reading Pane and choose Off rather than Right or Bottom, to avoid inadvertently reading spam or phishing emails.

Don't forget

Click the < arrow to collapse the Folder pane (or the > arrow to expand it). Click the More Options (...) on Navigation Options for Notes, Folders and Shortcuts.

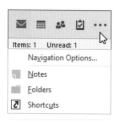

5 If you do want to set up Outlook Mobile on your phone, tick the box before clicking OK

6 Enter your phone number and click Send link to enable you to complete Setup on the phone

7 Outlook opens on the Desktop with Mail selected and with the most recent message displayed

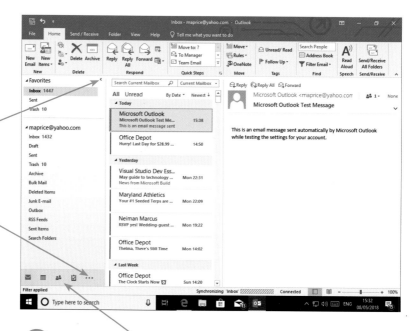

8 There are buttons to switch to the Mail, Calendar, People and Tasks views, plus More Options (...) for more links

9 Internet

Windows 10 provides two internet browsers to help you navigate through the web – the Universal app, Microsoft Edge; and the Classic app, Internet Explorer. They share many features but offer some unique options; e.g. Web Notes in Microsoft Edge, and RSS Feed subscriptions in Internet Explorer.

Internet Connection

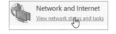

Alternatively, open the Control Panel and click View network status and tasks, from Network and Internet.

If your computer is connected to your DSL router (usually provided by your internet service provider) via an Ethernet cable, the connections will usually be set up automatically when you install Windows 10, or the first time that you use a computer with Windows 10 pre-installed.

If you have a wireless connection to your router, you'll be asked to provide the network key the first time, but the connection will be automatic thereafter.

To review your network settings:

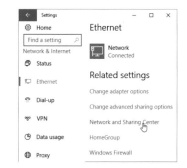

1 Open Settings, select the Network & Internet group and click Ethernet

2 Select Network and Sharing Center

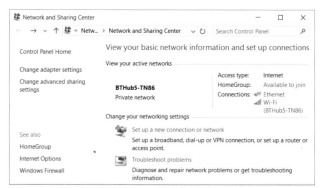

In this example, there are two connections – Ethernet (cable) and Wi-Fi (wireless). Each provides access to the internet, and is defined as a Private network.

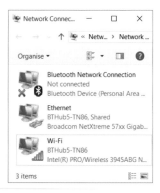

3 Click Change adapter settings in the Network and Sharing Center for details of the connections available

...cont'd

To set up a new internet connection directly from your computer:

1 In the Network and Sharing Center, select the link to Set up a new connection or network

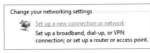

Change your networking settings

Set up a new connection or network
Set up a broadband, dial-up, or VPN connection; or set up a router or access point.

2 Choose Connect to the Internet to start the wizard, which prompts you to select the connection type

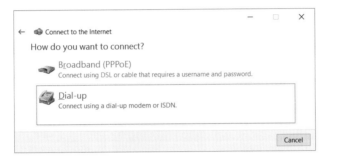

Connect to the Internet
Set up a broadband or dial-up connection to the Internet

Connect to the Internet

How do you want to connect?

Broadband (PPPoE)
Connect using DSL or cable that requires a username and password.

Dial-up
Connect using a dial-up modem or ISDN.

Cancel

3 Click the type, and then depending on your choice, provide a phone number (dial-up only), username and password, then click Create

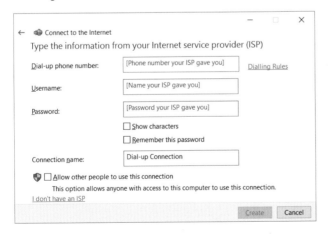

Connect to the Internet

Type the information from your Internet service provider (ISP)

Dial-up phone number: [Phone number your ISP gave you]   Dialling Rules

Username: [Name your ISP gave you]

Password: [Password your ISP gave you]
                            ☐ Show characters
                            ☐ Remember this password

Connection name: Dial-up Connection

🛡 ☐ Allow other people to use this connection
     This option allows anyone with access to this computer to use this connection.
I don't have an ISP

                                              Create   Cancel

Click the box to allow anyone with access to the computer to use the connection. Clear the box to reserve the connection for use with your account only.

Don't forget

If your network wasn't available at the time of installation, you can add a connection later.

Don't forget

If there's already an internet connection the wizard will tell you, but will allow you to continue and set up a second connection; for example, a dial-up backup for your DSL connection.

→ Set up a new connection anyway

Browse the Web

By default, Windows 10 provides access to the internet via Edge: the new browser from Microsoft. Internet Explorer v11.0 is also available, for websites that do not work with Edge.

1 Click the Microsoft Edge icon on the Taskbar to open the app

Don't forget

If you are running Windows 10 in Tablet mode, icons are not normally displayed on the Taskbar, so select the Microsoft Edge tile from the Start menu.

You can also start Microsoft Edge from the All Apps list.

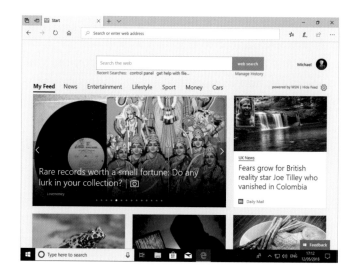

2 The Start screen displays, with a News channel provided by MSN. Scroll down for more items

Don't forget

You can scroll the screen with the mouse wheel, with the scroll bar that appears when you move the mouse, or by dragging the scroll bar on a touch monitor.

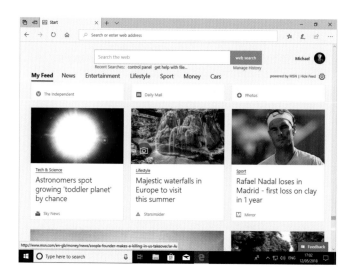

3 Click in the Search box at the top of the Start screen and begin typing your search term; for example, "bbc" to see related Search suggestions

The Hub (see pages 166-167) gives access to the Favorites, Reading List, History and Downloads.

4 Choose one of the Search suggestions, for example "bbc news", to see the list of web pages matching that particular term

More Options (...) gives access to a variety of options.

5 Select one of the web pages and explore the commands that are available

Back Forward Refresh Home New Tab Address Bar

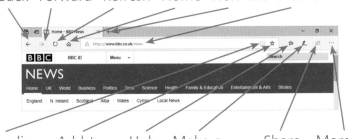

Reading View   Add to Favorites   Hub   Make a Web Note   Share   More Options

(...................These are called Toolbar buttons...................)

Reading View

Reading View transforms a web page into a simple format that has less distractions – no sidebars, ads, comments, etc.

1 Below is an example of a web page that has Reading View enabled

2 To enable Reading View, click the Reading View icon (or press Ctrl + Shift + R)

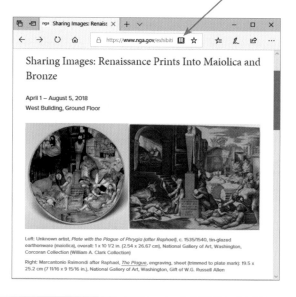

Settings

1 To configure Microsoft Edge, select More Options (...) and then Settings

Choose a theme
You can have the default Light theme or the Dark theme (see page 164).

Open Microsoft Edge with
You can choose the Start page (see page 160), a New tab page, Previous pages, or a Specific page or pages. There's also a Homepage button (see page 161).

Open new tabs with
Click the box to switch between Top sites and a blank page when opening new tabs.

Favorites bar
Click the button to turn it on and show the Favorites bar, where you can add selected sites (see pages 166-167).

1 Click View advanced settings to review other settings available

Import favorites and other information from any other browser you may have installed.

You can clear browsing data that may build up on your system, by selecting Choose what to clear in Settings.

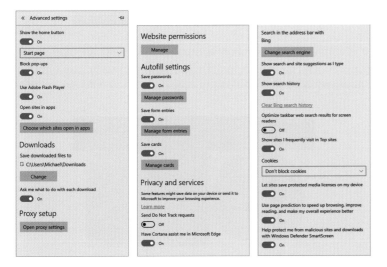

Light and Dark Themes

Microsoft Edge offers a choice of two display themes:

1 Open a web page and the default Light theme will be applied to all displayed Microsoft Edge menus; for example, History:

Hot tip

You can switch to the high-contrast Dark theme if it makes it easier for you to view web pages.

2 From More Options (...), Settings, pick Dark from the Choose a theme drop-down list

Don't forget

Press Ctrl + Shift + O to reveal the web page toolbar, where you can change text size and spacing, font style and page theme.

The selected theme is immediately applied to all displayed menus. Note the contents of the displayed web page are in no way affected by your choice of theme for Microsoft Edge.

Left: Unknown artist, *Plate with the Plague of Phrygia (after Raphael)*, c. 1535/1540, tin-glazed earthenware (maiolica), overall: 1 x 10 1/2 in. (2.54 x 26.67 cm), National Gallery of Art, Washington, Corcoran Collection (William A. Clark Collection)

Web Notes

1 Open a web page that you'd like to annotate and click the New Web Note button

Microsoft Edge lets you take notes, write, draw and highlight directly on web pages as a note that you can save or share.

2 The Web Notes toolbar is added, including pen options, text boxes (Note), Save and Share

The tools that are provided include:

Pen

Highlighter

Eraser

Note

Clip

3 Tap the Pen or Highlighter icons to write or highlight items on the web page, or tap Note to type text

4 Select Save, click OneNote (no name), Favorites or Reading list (check name), then click Save

Click the X button to Exit and leave Web Note mode.

The Hub

The Hub is the place where Microsoft Edge keeps all of the things you collect on the web.

1 Select Hub from the Toolbar buttons (see page 161) and it opens, initially with Favorites selected

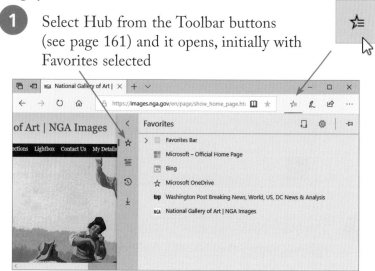

2 Click Reading List to view the list of pages you have added, plus any Web Notes you have created

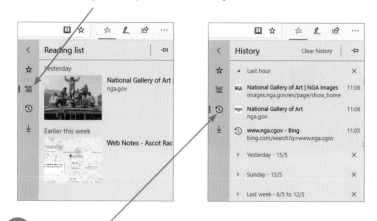

3 Select History to see the list of websites and web pages you have visited, organized by time and date

4 Click the white triangle (▷) next to a time or date to see the individual web pages visited during that period (it becomes a black triangle (◢) to show the list is expanded)

Don't forget

To add a web page to your Favorites list, click the Add to favorites (spellings are localized) button while viewing the page. You can save the page in Favorites or on the Favorites bar, or create a folder to organize your pages.

Hot tip

You can also use the Add to favorites button and select Reading list to put the current web page in the Reading List.

5 Click Downloads to view the list of files that you have downloaded in the past

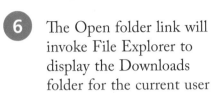

6 The Open folder link will invoke File Explorer to display the Downloads folder for the current user

The Downloads folder is the location where your downloaded files are usually stored, though they may be deleted after use; for example, upon program installation.

7 To remove the Hub area, click anywhere outside of it to close it

8 To fix the Hub in view, click the Pin button and it is displayed alongside the web page

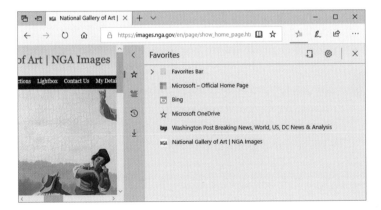

9 When you do want to hide the Hub pane, click the Close button

10 The next time you display the Hub pane, it will open in the area last viewed and it will be unpinned

The Downloads section shows the downloads that were managed through Microsoft Edge. Other browsers may also add files to the Downloads folder.

167

This shows the Favorites bar, which is a folder within the Favorites (note the spellings are localized).

Microsoft Edge enhancements, including improved speed and increased battery life, are included in the Windows 10 Creators Update.

Right-click Menus

Hot tip

You can view multiple pages in Microsoft Edge, each on a separate tab (see page 172).

Don't forget

Hyperlinks direct you to other website locations. They can be associated with images, graphics and text.

1 Open a selection of web pages in Microsoft Edge

2 Right-click an empty part of the page (the mouse pointer remains as an arrow) to get a basic context menu

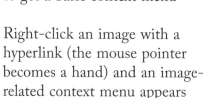

3 Right-click an image with a hyperlink (the mouse pointer becomes a hand) and an image-related context menu appears

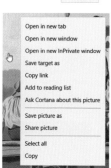

4 There's a more restricted context menu displayed when you right-click text with a hyperlink (again with a hand pointer)

These right-click actions are quite unlike those you get with the Internet Explorer Classic app. To view the differences:

1 Select one of the tabs (see page 172) in Microsoft Edge

2 Select the More Options button from the Toolbar and choose Open with Internet Explorer

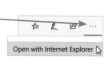

...cont'd

The web page on the current tab in the Universal app Microsoft Edge is displayed in the Classic app Internet Explorer.

3 Right-click a plain part of the web page, or one of the hyperlinks, and see the various menus that are displayed:

Plain Area | Background Patterned Area | Picture Hyperlink | Text Hyperlink

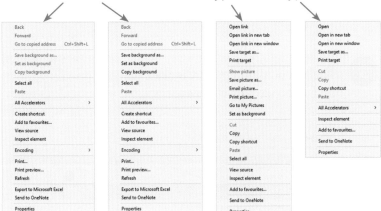

4 Right-click alongside the tabs, in the clear space between the New tab button and the Home button, to see the menu that controls which parts of Internet Explorer are enabled

Only the active tab from Microsoft Edge is opened initially, though you can add more tabs and switch between web pages as usual.

There may be slight differences on some systems, depending on what is installed, but the menus shown here are typical.

Internet Explorer can display Menu, Favorites, Command and Status bars, and show tabs on a separate row.

Desktop Internet Explorer

Don't forget

The browser icon on the Taskbar opens the Microsoft Edge app, but you can add the icon for Internet Explorer to the Taskbar as well.

Hot tip

Select one bar at a time, and it is added and then marked with a tick. Select again to remove the tick and hide the bar. You can also set Show tabs on a separate row.

1 Select Internet Explorer from All Apps, Windows Accessories

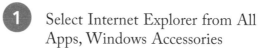

2 Internet Explorer opens in a window on the Homepage

Address and Search Bar   Tab Bar   New Tab   Mini Toolbar

Back and Forward Arrows

Search Button

Web Page Content

Text Links

3 Right-click alongside the Tab bar to add another bar; e.g. Favorites

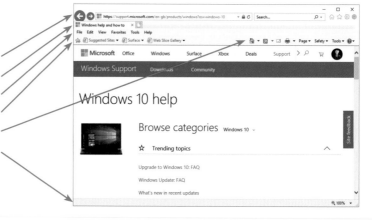

Back and Forward
Tab Bar
Menu Bar
Favorites Bar
Command Bar
Status Bar

4 Click in the Address bar, and Internet Explorer makes suggestions based on your previous visits

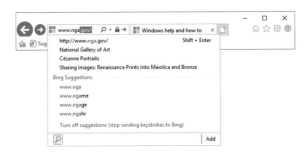

5 Click a hyperlink to switch to that web page

When you move the mouse pointer over a hyperlink and the hand symbol appears, you may see an image description. You'll also see the address the hyperlink points to.

George Caleb Bingham The Jolly Flatboatmen (2015.18.1)
https://images.nga.gov/en/search/do_quick_search.html

6 Click the Back and Forward buttons to review pages

The web page history associated with the Forward and Back arrows helps you to return to locations you have recently visited.

7 Right-click Back/Forward to view and select from the list of your recent visits, or select History for previous visits

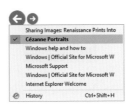

Tabbed Browsing

Using tabbed browsing allows you to explore more websites simultaneously, without losing your place in the website you are currently viewing.

There are several ways to create a new tab:

1 Click the New Tab button, and a new tab is added as the active tab

2 Press Ctrl + T, and a new tab is added and again becomes the active tab

3 Right-click a hyperlink and select Open in new tab. A tab with that web page is added, but it does not become the active tab

These keyboard shortcuts apply to both Internet Explorer and Microsoft Edge. When you have web pages open in both browsers:

4 Select Task View on the Taskbar to see each browser with its active tab

5 Move the mouse over the Taskbar browser icons

For Microsoft Edge, there's just one thumbnail for the active tab. Internet Explorer has thumbnails for all of its open tabs.

Zoom Web Page

You may find some web pages difficult to read, especially if you have your monitor set for high resolution. There are several ways to magnify a web page in Internet Explorer:

Hot tip

Values below 100% are useful as an overview for large web pages. Choose Custom... to apply a specific zoom factor. You can specify any value between 10% and 1000%.

1 Click the Tools button, select Zoom and choose a level; e.g. 100%

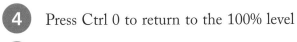

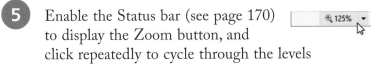

2 Press Ctrl + to Zoom in, 25% more each time

3 Press Ctrl - to Zoom out, 25% less each time

4 Press Ctrl 0 to return to the 100% level

5 Enable the Status bar (see page 170) to display the Zoom button, and click repeatedly to cycle through the levels

Microsoft Edge also provides a Zoom feature. Its methods for zooming the web page include:

1 Select More Options (...) and on the Zoom entry click the + or - buttons to zoom in or out, 25% at a time

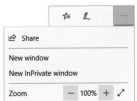

2 Press Ctrl + to Zoom in, or Ctrl - to Zoom out, again 25% more each time

3 Press Ctrl 0 to return to 100%

There are no menus of scale factors, and no custom scaling.

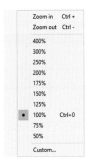

Don't forget

Click the down-arrow next to the Internet Explorer Zoom button to display the Zoom menu and select the level required.

RSS Feeds

Internet Explorer tells you whenever there's an RSS feed available, if you enable the Command bar to see the Feeds icon.

An RSS feed (also known as a web feed) is a means of collating updates to web pages so you can be made aware of changes without having to revisit the website.

1 If there are no feeds available, the button is grayed out

2 When you switch to a web page that has a feed, the Feeds button changes color and a sound may play

Microsoft Edge does not support RSS. However, if you have Microsoft Office, you can use Outlook 2016 as your RSS reader. Right-click the RSS Feeds folder and select Add a New RSS Feed.

3 Click the down-arrow to the side of the Feeds button and select the feed to view reports it offers

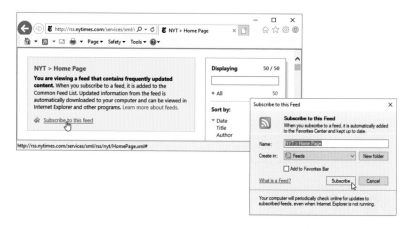

4 If the reports interest you, click Subscribe to this feed then click Subscribe, and you'll be able to view updated content in Internet Explorer or in your Outlook 2016 email app

10 Windows Games

You can access Xbox Games or the Microsoft Store, to find a variety of products to challenge and teach. Record your scores and compare your results with friends, or other players.

Games in Windows 10

In previous releases of Windows, a good selection of games was included in the initial installation. In Windows 7, for example, you'd find the following in the Games folder:

Associated with this folder was the Games Explorer, which helped you to get software updates and news feeds for the installed games. The Games Explorer also tracked wins, losses and other statistics.

However, you won't find these games in Windows 10, since they are not pre-installed, and there's only a few Universal game apps, such as the Microsoft Solitaire Collection. However, you will find many games available at the Microsoft Store (see page 128). These include many free games, though you should be aware that there may be in-app purchases suggested during play.

Microsoft has integrated Xbox content and gaming services into Windows 10, and provides the Xbox app (see page 186). This gives Windows 10 players access to the Xbox Live network, so they can keep track of their achievements, see what their friends are playing, and participate in multi-player games. Xbox One users are also able to stream their Xbox games to their Windows 10 PC or Tablet.

Games at the Microsoft Store

1 Open the Microsoft Store and select Games, to see sample games and links to selections, such as Top games and Featured games

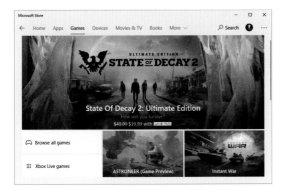

The games that are featured and the games selected for each list will change frequently, but these examples illustrate the type of findings you can expect.

2 Scroll down to see a selection of Top paid games

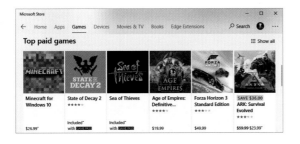

Click the Show all link for any selection, to browse the complete set of games in that group.

3 Scroll on to find the selection of Best selling games

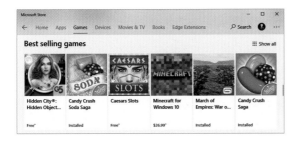

Best sellers include Free as well as Chargeable games. Microsoft Store also identifies games you have installed.

...cont'd

Hot tip

If you have a narrow window, you can scroll the selection horizontally using the arrow box displayed as you move the mouse to the edge.

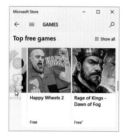

Hot tip

Individual games may appear in several groups. For example, games shown in the Top free or Top paid selections may also be included in the Trending or Collections selection.

④ Scroll on, using the vertical scroll bar or the mouse wheel, and review the selection of Top free games (and click Show all to explore the complete set)

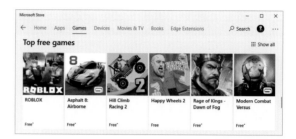

⑤ You can also explore the various Collections of games, or view the selection of Best-rated games

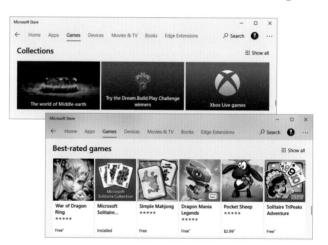

⑥ Scroll downwards to the bottom of the Games page and you can select games by category

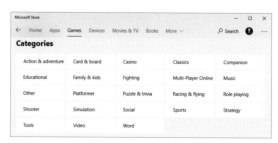

Word Games

1 Go to the Store, and search for games under the term "word search". Our search found 128 such games

Word Search
★★★★★
🖥 ▢
Free*

Get

2 Select the entry Word Search by Steve Nessen, and follow the prompts to install the app on your system

Don't forget

You can choose games that are complex and challenging, such as Mahjong and Solitaire, or you can choose simple games that are easy and fun to play, such as the Word Games collection.

3 Open Word Search from the All Apps list

Word Search
New

4 Select Settings and choose the difficulty level and the types of word list

5 Click the back arrow to exit Settings

6 Select Start, and play the game. At the Easy level, words are vertical or horizontal, and you can see a scrolling list of the words you are looking for

7 When you have located all the words, the game ends and your score is displayed

Hot tip

Select Highscore to see a list of your results, and select Trophies to set yourself some challenges.

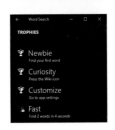

Microsoft Solitaire Collection

Don't forget

If you have enjoyed playing FreeCell or Spider Solitaire in a previous release of Windows, you'll be pleased to find the Microsoft Solitaire Collection in the Store.

Hot tip

By signing in and creating an Xbox profile (see page 186), you can record the results for all the games you play and share your achievements with other players.

Don't forget

You will also have access to the Daily Challenges, Awards, Achievements and Statistics.

1 Find the game in the Microsoft Store, and note that it is already installed on your system

2 Select the Store entry to see its description

You are advised that there are in-app purchase options.

3 Select Play from the Store entry (or select the Start menu entry) and click X to clear the initial message

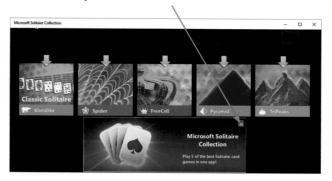

4 The app loads up and offers you the choice of Klondike, Spider, FreeCell, Pyramid and TriPeaks

5 Click Menu, Themes to see the themes for the playing cards, and then tap to download extra themes

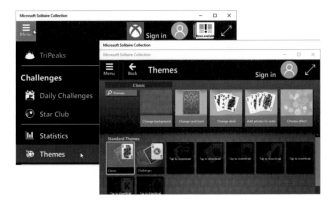

Don't forget

The Theme specifies the card deck style and the play area background for all of the games in the collection.

6 Select a game, e.g. FreeCell, and choose a level of play. There's an optional tutorial on how to play the game. Click Next to view the tutorial

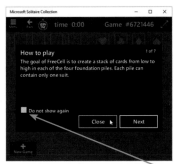

Hot tip

Click the Do not show again box to avoid loading the tutorial when you open the game in future.

7 Click Close to leave the tutorial and play the game

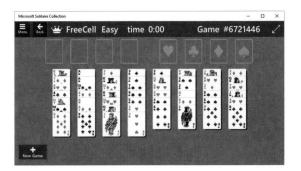

Microsoft Minesweeper

The process that you follow to install and play Minesweeper is typical for Xbox games on Windows 10 PCs.

1 Find Microsoft Minesweeper in the Microsoft Store to view the description (noting the in-app purchases)

2 Click Get and follow the prompts to install the game, and choose to Pin to Start if you wish to add the related tile to the Start menu

3 Select the tile, or locate the app from the All Apps list, to open the game

The first time you play, you'll be asked to allow the game to access and update the Xbox Live information for the Xbox gamertag associated to your Microsoft account (see tip on page 186).

You could also open the game from the Play button that now shows on the Microsoft Store entry for the game.

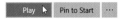

4 Choose one of the game types such as Easy 9x9 to get started, or a more advanced level depending on your experience and ability

5 A board at the selected level is prepared, ready for you to play

6 The first time you play, you are offered an optional tutorial with hints and prompts to explain how it works. You can either skip this or go through the tutorial

You use the number displayed to help deduce whether a square is safe to uncover. Right-click a suspect square to add a flag, or left-click a safe cell. On a touchscreen, you would press and hold for a flag, or tap for a safe cell.

7 The first click is safe, but after that you must check carefully before selecting a cell as safe or potentially mined

8 If you go wrong the results will be explosive, and the game will terminate

Open the Xbox app (see page 186) and select Achievements from the menu to see the results for the recent games you have played.

9 Get it right, and you are treated to fireworks at the end of the game

10 Your scores are recorded and made available to the Xbox app (and your Xbox gamertag) so they can be shared with other players

Microsoft Mahjong

Don't forget

This game has four skill levels, with about a dozen puzzles for each, giving 51 in total. It can be played with keyboard, mouse or by touch.

1 Locate the game in the Store, and click the Get button to install it, then pin it to the Start menu if required

2 Select the Tile for the game (or select the All Apps entry)

3 The first time you play the game, you are asked for permission to access your Xbox Live info associated with your Xbox gamertag

4 Select Choose puzzle

5 You start off with one Easy puzzle unlocked

Hot tip

As with all the Xbox Live games, you get a record of your scores for all the puzzles, and you can compare your results with other players using the Xbox gamertag associated with your Microsoft account.

6 Each time you complete a puzzle in a group, the next one will be unlocked and available to play

7 Select the new puzzle, or choose to replay a previous puzzle

...cont'd

8 Click matching pairs of free tiles to remove them

9 If you get stuck, press H for a hint, and two matching tiles will flash

10 Fireworks are displayed when you complete the game, and the next puzzle gets unlocked

11 Click OK, and your results will be recorded in your Xbox info

The first time you play, you are offered a tutorial to help you learn the basic operations of the game. You can skip the tutorial if you wish.

Tutorial
Welcome to Microsoft Mahjong! Let's take a minute to learn the basics of the game.

Teach me how to play   Skip the tutorial

You can choose the newly unlocked puzzle, replay a previous puzzle, or move up to the next level.

Xbox App

The Xbox app manages scores for Windows 10 versions of Xbox games. You do not have to own an Xbox games device.

1 Click the Xbox tile on the Start menu and Xbox opens with your gamertag

2 Click the Menu button and select My Games to list Windows 10 Xbox games installed on your system

3 Select Menu, Achievements to see the results for the Xbox games you have played

4 To add more Xbox games, search the Store using the term "Xbox", and you'll find quite a number of games. Our search found 271 games

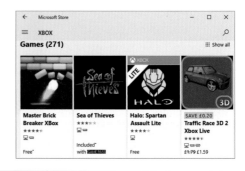

5 Install the ones you want to try

11 Music and Pictures

With the integrated sound card in your system, you can create recordings, play CDs and convert tracks to computer files to manage within your music and sound library. You can also manage Movie and TV show collections, and create albums and slideshows from digital images and photos.

Sound Card and Speakers

The sound card in your computer processes the information from apps such as Groove Music or Cortana and sends audio signals to your computer's speakers.

To review and adjust your sound setup:

1 Open the Control Panel from Windows System on the All Apps list (see page 78 for other methods)

2 Select Hardware and Sound (View by: Category) and then Sound

see page 78 for other methods

3 Click the Playback tab, select the entry for Speakers, then click Configure

4 Select your speaker setup, click Test to check the speakers, and then click Next to continue

Click Test to hear a sound from each speaker, or click an individual speaker to hear a sound from it, to ensure all speakers are working.

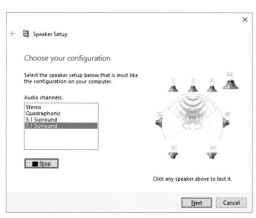

The sound card on your system will usually be incorporated into the system board, or may be provided as a separate adapter card.

5 Specify which speakers are present in your setup

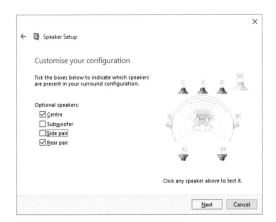

6 Specify if speakers are full-range versus satellite

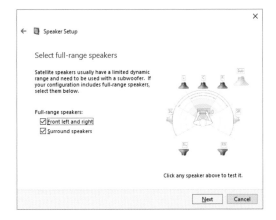

7 Click Finish to complete and apply the new settings to your computer

If you have a laptop or tablet PC with built-in speakers, these will normally be stereo and full-range types.

Satellite speakers are external and normally small, discreet and cannot play low-frequency sounds. They're usually paired with a subwoofer.

If you have a separate sound adapter, it may be installed with its own audio application program to set up, configure and test the device features.

Recording

In this example, there are two microphones: one a headset and the other a webcam.

With a sound card in your system, you can make voice recordings from a microphone or other audio sources. To set up your microphone:

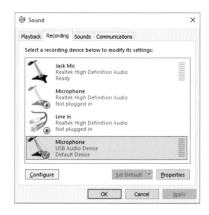

1 From the Control Panel, Sound option, click on the Recording tab

2 Select the Microphone entry, then click Configure

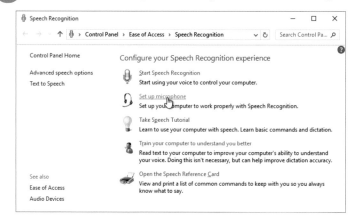

3 Select Set up microphone and select the type you are using (headset, desktop or another kind)

There are several types of microphone in common use, but a headset microphone is the best choice if you are considering the use of voice control.

4 You should set up your microphone according to the recommendations, to ensure clear and effective recordings

5 Read the sample text and follow the prompts to set up the microphone for the best recording quality

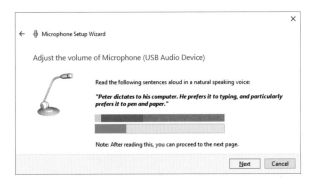

If there are problems with the level of recording, you may be asked to go back and try again, perhaps avoiding background noise.

6 Your microphone is now set up. Click Finish

Repeat the microphone configuration in Step 2 and take the Speech Tutorial, to train your computer to better understand your voice.

With the microphone set up, you can now use a program such as Voice Recorder, installed with Windows 10, to record and play audio notes and memos with the single click of a button.

The recordings you make can be stored on your OneDrive, so you can share and access them from any computer.

When you've set up your microphone and speakers, you'll be able to use the Cortana Digital Assistant to ask questions and get audio responses.

Play Audio CD

Don't forget

You also use your sound adapter and speakers to play music from a CD or files that you download from the internet.

1 Insert an audio CD and close the drive

2 Windows recognizes the type of disc and prompts you (if a default action isn't yet defined)

DVD RW Drive (F:) Audio CD
Tap to choose what happens with audio CDs.

3 You can choose to Play audio CD (using Windows Media Player) or Take no action, whenever audio CDs are inserted

DVD RW Drive (F:) Audio CD

Choose what to do with audio CDs.

Play audio CD
Windows Media Player

Take no action

4 Click Play audio CD. Windows Media Player starts, and the first time you must choose the settings

5 Select Recommended settings, or click Custom settings to review, and if necessary make changes to the Privacy options that are applied

Don't forget

If you accept the recommendations, Windows Media Player becomes the default for music files. Information about the music is downloaded and usage data will be sent to Microsoft if you select the Customer Experience Improvement Program box.

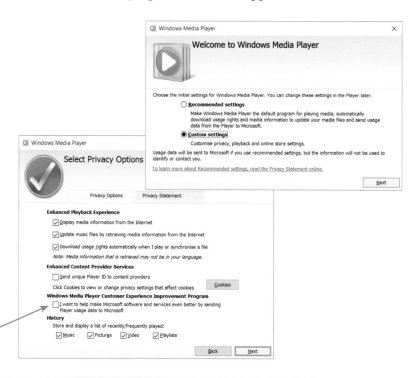

...cont'd

6 Make Windows Media Player the default, or choose the file types that you want it to handle

Windows Media Player is the only option offered for playing CDs. However, to play music files there is also the Groove Music app (see pages 196-197).

7 The CD begins to play in a mini Windows Media Player screen and track data is added

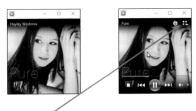

8 Move the mouse over the window and then click the Switch to Library button that appears, to see your Windows Media Player Library, and the CD details

The CD provides the track numbers and the durations, and if you have an internet connection the CD is identified, and the full artist and album details are downloaded.

193

Copy Tracks

Beware

The higher the bit rate, the better the quality but the larger the file. As an estimate, a full audio disc copied at:

Bit rate	Needs
128 Kbps	57 MB
192 Kbps	86 MB
256 Kbps	115 MB
320 Kbps	144 MB

Don't forget

You can choose if you want copy protection on your music, but in any event you must confirm you understand the copyright nature of the material.

1 Right-click the Now Playing window, select More Options..., then click the Rip Music tab

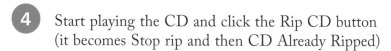

2 For Format, choose the type of audio file (e.g. MP3)

3 Choose the Audio quality (e.g. using bit rate 192 Kbps)

4 Start playing the CD and click the Rip CD button (it becomes Stop rip and then CD Already Ripped)

5 Each track in turn is copied, converted and saved

6 Files will be saved by default in your Music folder, and the CD can play while tracks are being copied

Media Library

The converted tracks will be saved in the specified location (the Music folder) on your hard drive, in an album under the artist's name.

Type "Windows media" on the Start menu, then press Enter. If you plan to use this often, you can Pin it to the Taskbar or the Start menu (see page 69).

To explore the albums stored on your hard drive and to play tracks from them:

1 Start the Windows Media Player and click the Library button to switch to the Library view

2 You can choose how to display the contents of the Music library; e.g. by Album, by Artist, or by Genre

3 Double-click an artist to display their albums, then double-click one of the albums to start it playing

Groove Music App

1 Select Groove Music from the Start menu to launch this Universal app

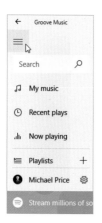

2 Groove Music gets ready then searches on your system to locate music files

3 The app can access music on your local drive or on your OneDrive, making it possible to play your music on more than one system

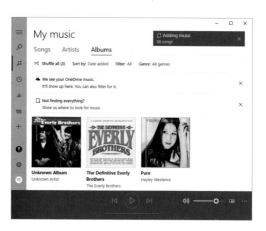

4 All the albums found in the default locations will be displayed. You can review the locations and amend them if desired

5 To search for more music, select Show us where to look for music (see image for Step 4)

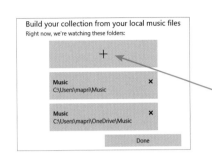

6 In this case, Groove Music looks at the current user's Music folders in the Library and on the OneDrive

You can click the Add button to specify another folder that contains music, or just click Done if you've finished reviewing the locations.

7 Click Filter and choose to display items that are Only on this device

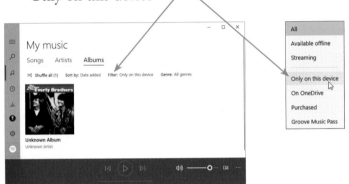

8 To change the display style, click the Settings icon and set Mode to Dark or Light (or system setting)

You can play albums that are on OneDrive on any device where you sign in with your Microsoft Account.

9 This is Dark style, with filter set to On OneDrive

Playing Music

1 In the Groove Music app, right-click an album, click the Select button and choose an album. A command bar appears, with a More Options (...) button if it is needed to display any additional commands

2 Click Play to hear the songs on the album, and click Show now playing list to see the songs available

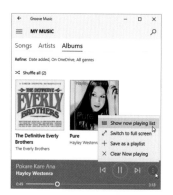 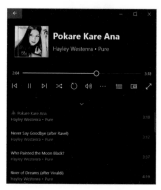

In either view, the Play controls are displayed: drag the play indicator to advance the song or replay; go forward to the next song or back to the previous one; and pause or resume play.

3 Select the Speaker icon and drag the slider to increase or decrease the volume

Hot tip

The Play controls also provide Repeat (to automatically restart the album when it completes playing) and Shuffle (to play the songs on the album in random order).

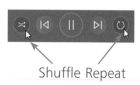

Shuffle   Repeat

4 Click the Stream millions icon, and it changes to Get Spotify, the free music streaming app

5 Select Get and Spotify is installed, and you can Sign up free (or Log In with an existing Spotify account)

6 Explore Spotify features such as Radio, Podcasts, Charts, Genre, Playlists, New releases and Concerts

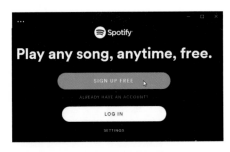

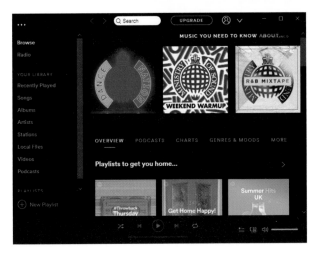

Hot tip

Microsoft has ended Groove Music Pass music streaming and Microsoft Store no longer sells music, with Spotify being the replacement.

Hot tip

You can Join Spotify using your Facebook ID or with your Email account and password.

Don't forget

You can play albums that are on OneDrive on any device where you sign in with your Microsoft Account.

Movies & TV

Hot tip

You can also add movie and TV content to your Windows 10 computer or mobile device by downloading from YouTube, or purchasing or renting from the Microsoft Store.

Don't forget

The Movies & TV app may be called Films & TV in some regions.

Hot tip

Click the links to see the specified selections, or simply scroll the Explore page to see subsets of each.

1 Select the Movies & TV tile from the Start menu to start the app

2 The app opens with Explore selected, showing featured movies. Select Trailers for more movies, or choose 360^0 videos to see examples of these

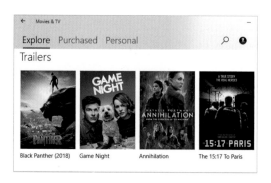

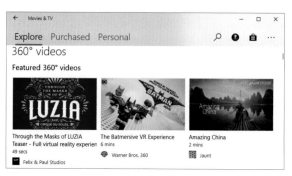

You can also explore selections of Movies and TV, or you can review your Purchased items and your Personal items.

...cont'd

3 Click Settings to set download quality (HD or SD)

4 Select Choose where we look for videos, to specify which libraries or folders the app should search

Settings

Download quality
○ HD
○ SD
◉ Ask every time

Download Location
Modify your storage settings

Download devices
Show my download devices
Remove this device
Learn more

Your videos
Restore my available video purchases
Choose where we look for videos

Account
View account
Payment options
Order history

Privacy
Export my purchased video info
Delete my purchased video info
View privacy dashboard

App
Help
Feedback
About
What's new

Build your collection from your local video files
Right now, we're watching these folders:

+

Videos
C:\Users\mapri\Videos ✕

Done

The Movies & TV app supports most DRM-free video formats, including:
- .m4v   .mp4
- .mov   .asf
- .avi   .wmv
- .m2ts   .3g2
- .3gp2   .3gpp

5 Click the Microsoft Store icon to open the Store with the Movies & TV selections

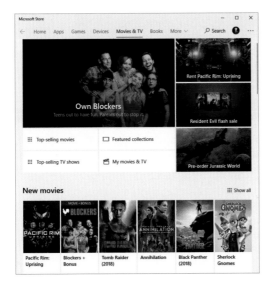

Scroll down to see selections of New, Top selling and Featured movies and TV shows, and you can also search for movies by genre.

6 Review the content, and purchase and install any items that you desire

Digital Pictures

There are a number of ways you can obtain digital pictures:

- Internet (e.g. saving images from art or photography websites).
- Scanner (copies of documents, photographs or slides).
- Digital Camera (photographs and movies).
- Email attachments and faxes.

Website pictures will usually be stored as JPEG (.jpg) files, which are compressed to minimize the file size. This preserves the full color range but there is some loss of quality. Some images such as graphic symbols and buttons will use the GIF (.gif) format, which restricts color to 256 shades to minimize the file size. To copy a digital image from a website such as **images.nga.gov**:

Microsoft Edge is used for this example, but you can do the same actions with Internet Explorer, though you do get different menus (see pages 168-169).

Hot tip

You can right-click and save the picture even when only part of it is visible on the screen.

1 Right-click the image, then select Save picture as

2 Accept (or amend) the file name, then click Save

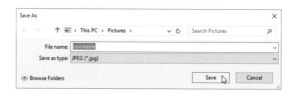

Hot tip

Click Browse Folders to select a folder and create a subfolder, e.g. using the artist name, to organize the saved images.

3 To view the saved images, go to the Start menu, click File Explorer, then Pictures, then select the appropriate sub-folder

4 To explore the folder more easily, select the View tab, then choose Extra large icons and Preview pane

5 Double-click an image to see it in the default picture viewer

6 Right-click the image, select Open with, then choose another app to see the default viewer and other options

Hot tip

To make more space in the folder, click the Navigation pane button and deselect that box.

Beware

Windows Photo Viewer is offered on systems that have been upgraded to Windows 10 from a previous version of Windows. It is not made available on fresh installs of Windows 10.

Photos App

Don't forget

Click the See more (...) icon on the command bar to display additional options to deal with photos.

Hot tip

Click the double-headed arrow at the bottom right-hand corner to expand to full screen.

Don't forget

You can click the Folders command to choose source folders from your local system or your OneDrive.

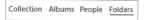

1 Double-click an image in your Pictures folders and the Photos app opens, showing the selected picture

2 Click the magnifying glass button to zoom

3 Click See all photos to see the contents of the picture folder, arranged in reverse chronological order

4 Click the Albums tab to see any albums that have been automatically created for you

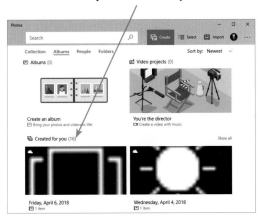

The Photos app will automatically organize your photographs (by date) into albums of related photos, choosing those it identifies as the best, although you can edit the selection.

5 Click See more (...), Settings and scroll through the list of facilities for managing the Photos app

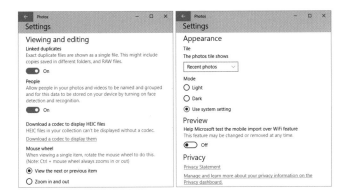

Click the X next to a folder to remove it from the Photos app. You'll be asked to confirm, and will be assured that the folder itself won't be deleted.

6 You can have duplicated files linked and shown as single entries, and use face recognition for people

7 In Settings, Sources, click Add a folder to specify where the Photos app finds content, and click the On/Off button for showing cloud-only content from OneDrive

Edit Pictures

Open a picture from your collection, and the toolbar across the top offers options to handle or adjust the image.

For further options for dealing with your photos, click See more (...) on the command bar.

1 Click the Edit and Create button to explore the effects (this will not change the original file)

2 Click the Edit command to view the filters offered by Enhance, or explore the Adjust commands

Hot tip

You can Adjust the Light, Color, Clarity and Vignette for your photo, and use the Red eye and Spot fix to handle blemishes.

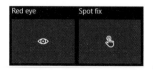

12 Networking

Create a home network, wired or wireless, to share drives, printers and internet access. Windows 10 computers can create or join a HomeGroup, to share content with other devices on the network.

Create a Network

You have a network when you have several devices that exchange information over a wire or over radio waves (wireless). The simplest network consists of one computer and a router that links to the internet. You can add a second computer, to share internet access and exchange information with the other computer. When the PCs are Windows 10-based, a HomeGroup can help share data.

Hot tip

Unlike devices that are attached directly to a computer, the devices on a network operate independently of one another.

This sample network map was created in Windows 7. There's no map in Windows 10, but it does show network devices (see page 214).

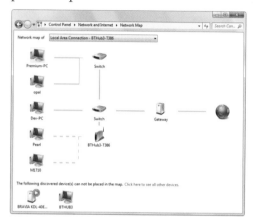

To make connections like these, your system will require components of the following types:

- Ethernet twisted-pair cables, for the wired portion.
- A router to manage the network connections.
- An internet modem, which may be integrated with the router.
- An adapter for each computer (wired or wireless).

To implement your network, you'll need to carry out actions such as these:

- Install the necessary network adapters.
- Establish the internet connection.
- Set up the wireless router.
- Connect the computers and start Windows.

Don't forget

Windows 10 detects the presence of a network and will automatically set up the computer to participate in and, for private networks, to create or join a HomeGroup.

Network Classification

1 Install the network adapter (if required) and start up Windows (with no network connection)

2 In the Notification area, the Network icon shows Unavailable

3 Add a cable from adapter to router and the Network icon shows Connected

Windows will detect the network when you start your computer and give it a default classification, but you can override its choice.

4 Click the Network icon, select Network & Internet settings, click Ethernet and select the network name

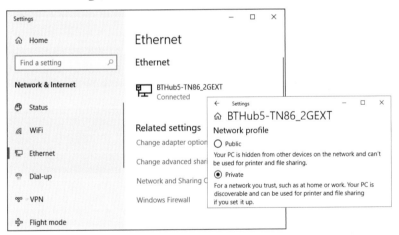

5 Select Private for personal networks (home or office), or select Public for shared networks (e.g. coffee shop, library, airport)

6 For wireless networks, click the Network icon, select Properties for the WiFi network, and switch between Public and Private as desired (see page 210)

see page 210

Don't forget

Often, there will be a network adapter built into your computer. If not, you'll need to install an adapter card or add a USB adapter.

Hot tip

For Ethernet, left-click the Network icon, then select Network & Internet settings.

Don't forget

Selecting Private lets you see other computers on the network and lets other network users see your computer. Selecting Public hides your computer, and you won't see other computers on the network.

Connect to a Wireless Network

Don't forget

Cabled PCs usually get added automatically. When you bring a new wireless PC into the network, you'll need to set up the connection.

Beware

Your system may detect other wireless networks that are in the vicinity, so make sure to select the correct entry.

Don't forget

Your computer will now always connect to that network when it comes into range. You can have numerous wireless connections defined; for example home, office and an internet café.

1 The Network icon on the right of the Taskbar shows Not connected - Connections are available

2 Click the icon to display the connections and select your main wireless network

3 Check the box to Connect automatically and then click Connect

4 Enter the network security key for your wireless network and click Next (or press the Router button to connect without entering the key)

5 Your computer is now shown as connected to the wireless network

6 If necessary, you can change the network type by selecting Properties from the WiFi Network Connection

7 Select Public or Private as required

View Network Devices

There's no network map in Windows 10, unlike Windows 7 (see page 208). However, you can display a list of computers and devices connected and active on the network.

1 Open the Control Panel in Category View and select Network and Internet

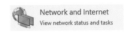

You can also go to the Desktop, open File Explorer from the Taskbar and select the Network category.

2 Find the entry for Network and Sharing Center and select the option to View network computers and devices

3 File Explorer opens at the Network section

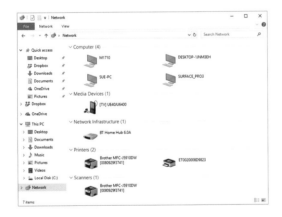

Only computers that have Network discovery turned on (see page 209) can find devices on the network, and only those devices that are currently active will show up.

4 Active computers and devices such as hubs, shared media libraries plus internet-connected TVs and recorders are shown

5 If Network discovery and File sharing are turned off, no devices are found. Click the banner to Turn on network discovery and file sharing to find devices

Network and Sharing Center

Hot tip

Alternatively, open the Network & Internet Settings (see page 213) and select Network and Sharing Center from the Related settings.

Related settings

Change adapter options

Change advanced sharing options

Network and Sharing Center

Windows Firewall

Hot tip

Select Change adapter settings to manage the networking adapters on your system.

Control Panel Home

Change adapter settings

Change advanced sharing settings

1 Open Control Panel, select Network and Internet and then select the entry for the Network and Sharing Center

Network and Sharing Center
View network status and tasks
Connect to a network
View network computers and devices

2 Here, you can view the basic information for your active networks

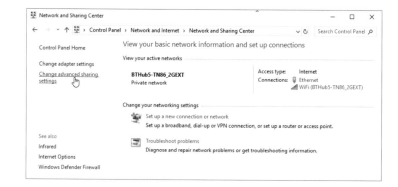

3 Click Change advanced sharing settings, to review the options for Private and for Public networks

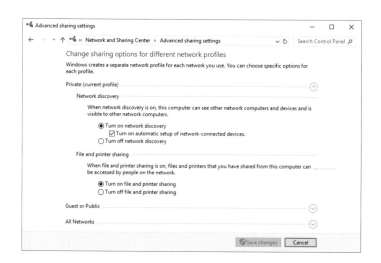

4 Click Save changes or Cancel as appropriate

Network & Internet Settings

1 Open Settings from the Start menu or Action Center, and select Network & Internet

2 Select WiFi or Ethernet, to see the options provided for these types of network

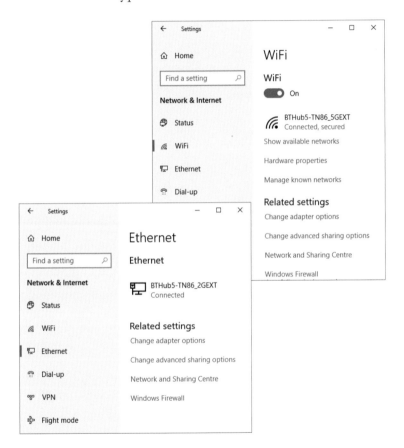

You can also click the Network icon in the Notification area and select Network & Internet settings, for your Ethernet or Wi-Fi connections.

When you select the Wi-Fi icon, you can enable Flight mode (see page 214) to manage your wireless broadband settings.

3 From here, you can choose to Change adapter options or to Change advanced sharing options

4 You can also open the Network and Sharing Center or select Windows Firewall to review network protection settings in the Windows Defender Security Center

Flight Mode

To avoid problems while flying or in secure environments such as hospitals, you may want to stop all wireless communications. You do this using Flight mode.

1. Open Network & Internet Settings and select the option for Flight mode, and the wireless devices on your system are shown

Don't forget

Until the April 2018 Update, the option was known as Airplane mode. This may still be the name shown on some systems, but the function is the same as Flight mode.

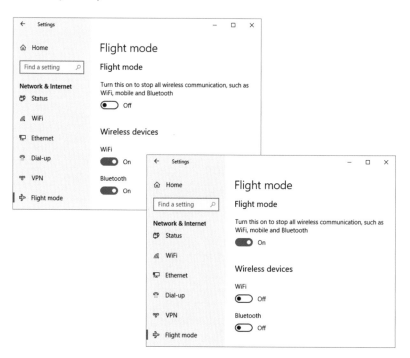

Hot tip

Only computers that have wireless devices will display Flight mode. It does not appear on systems with only Ethernet adapters, for example.

2. Select the button to turn on Flight mode, and all the wireless devices on your system are turned off

3. You can also turn Flight mode on or off when you left-click the network icon for a WiFi network

HomeGroup Ended

HomeGroup was introduced in Windows 7 to allow PCs on a local network to share files and printers with one another.

1 When you joined the network you could be invited to Create a homegroup, if there wasn't one already

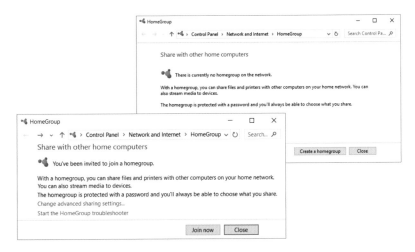

Don't forget

When your system installs the Windows 10 April 2018 Update, or any later update, you will find that HomeGroup no longer appears in File Explorer, Control Panel or Troubleshoot, and there will be no more invitations to Create or Join a HomeGroup.

2 If a HomeGroup already existed on the network, you would be invited to join

3 File Explorer would show the HomeGroup and let you access the members and their shared content

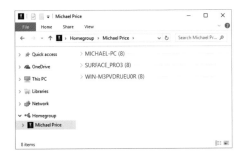

Hot tip

Windows 10 provides numerous features that will help you share files, folders and printers with other users and devices on your network.

All this changed with the April 2018 Update. In this update the HomeGroup feature was withdrawn, although any existing files, folders or printers previously shared with HomeGroup should continue to be shared. For any new sharing, you must use other Windows 10 features such as OneDrive.

HomeGroup Alternatives

If you have printers, folders or files you want to share with other users and devices on your network:

1 Open Settings and select Devices, Printers & scanners, click on the printer and select Manage

2 Pick Printer properties and the Sharing tab, check Share this printer, and confirm the Share name

3 Select a folder in File Explorer, click the Share tab and the Share button, then click Specific people and choose the users who can access that folder

4 Select a file, click Share and the Share button and choose the users who can get that file

Hot tip

You can use features of Windows 10 to share printers, files and folders on your private network.

Hot tip

You can also right-click the folder and select Give access to, Specific people.

Right-click a file and select Share to choose the users allowed.

Nearby Sharing

With the April 2018 Update, PCs can now send items such as files, links and photos to nearby PCs over Bluetooth.

1 Select Settings, System, Shared Experiences, and scroll down to Nearby sharing

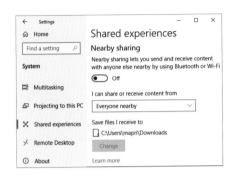

Hot tip

Nearby Sharing is similar to Apple's AirDrop. However, it will initially only work between two Windows 10 PCs that have the feature enabled. You can't yet share from mobile or other operating systems.

2 Click the On/Off button to turn on Nearby sharing, and you can share with Everybody nearby, or choose to limit sharing to My devices only

3 Open File Explorer, select the file you wish to share, click the Share tab and click the Share button

4 Any devices with Nearby sharing enabled are detected, and you can choose the one you want

5 Open the Action Center to confirm that Nearby sharing is enabled, and click the button to reset it Off or On

Beware

If Nearby sharing is not already enabled when you select a file to share, you'll be asked to Tap to turn on nearby sharing.

Mobile Hotspot

You can use the internet connection on your Windows 10 PC to allow devices to access the internet when the router is not accessible, or when you don't want to reveal your main network password, using Mobile hotspot:

1 Open Settings from the Start menu or Action Center and select Network & Internet, then click the Mobile hotspot entry

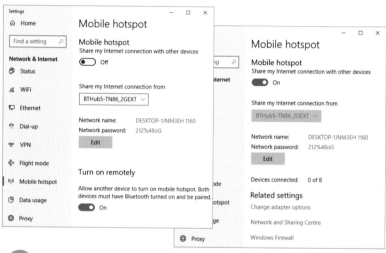

Hot tip

Here, a PC is able to identify two PCs on the network that are making their internet connections available via Mobile hotspot.

2 Click the Off/On button to turn on Mobile hotspot, and note the network name and password

3 If your PC has both Ethernet and WiFi, you can use either to support the Mobile hotspot

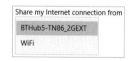

4 Note that if your PC has Ethernet only, and no WiFi, it will be unable to offer the Mobile hotspot facility

13 Security & Maintenance

Help and support is enhanced using the latest online information, as well as many other ways of getting useful advice. Windows Action Center keeps track of your system, and a variety of system tools help protect your computer from hazards.

Tips App

Included with Windows 10 is a Tips app to help you learn about the operating system, with detailed instructions, slideshows and videos covering a range of the features and functions of Windows 10.

1 Select Tips from All Apps, and the app opens with a number of sections

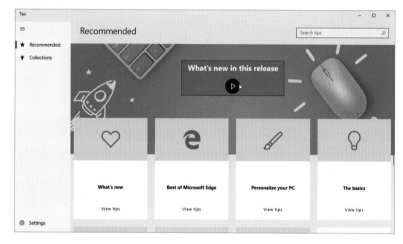

Recommended
This offers sets of tips covering what's new in Windows 10; features of Microsoft Edge; how to personalize your PC; and the basics of using Windows 10. Each topic has typically 6 to 12 tips presented in slide format.

What's new in this release
This slide presentation of What's new in Windows 10 highlights the latest features and acts as a lead in to the topics and tips provided in the Tips app.

More Topics

Scroll down to find more recommended topics, helping you to get organized, create and edit videos, and create in 3D. There's also an option to browse all tips, which actually displays the Collections component of the Tips app.

To access all the tips, you can select Browse all tips from Recommended, or select Collections.

Collections

This is the full set of tips, in five groups: Windows 10 (23 topics), Microsoft Edge (3 topics), Office (1 topic), Windows apps (5 topics) and Mixed reality (3 topic sets).

You can flag any tip to indicate This is helpful, or This is not helpful, and you can Share the tip with any of your contacts.

Select a group, choose a topic and review the tips it offers.

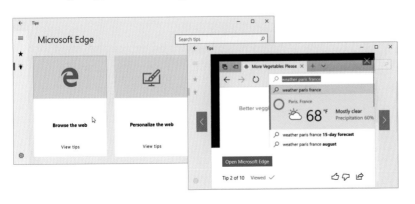

Don't forget

Windows 10 doesn't provide the local Help information found in earlier versions, but the Microsoft Support website has extensive help on all Microsoft products.

Hot tip

The topics suggested are based on your own setup and include, for example, computers and devices associated with your Microsoft Account.

Hot tip

Scroll on further to see other support topic areas, and for links to other useful websites.

Microsoft Support

If the Tips app does not answer your questions, you can review the information offered by Microsoft Support.

1 Open **http://support.microsoft.com**, type your search terms, and select one of the results

2 Alternatively, scroll further down the page and select one of the suggested products, based on your own setup, or choose View all Microsoft products

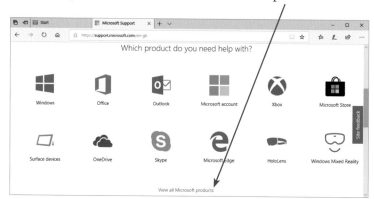

3 Review the products listed, and select the most appropriate. For example, choose Windows 10

...cont'd

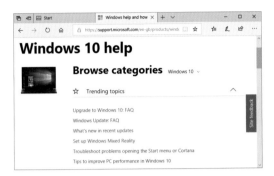

The topics presented will be the most currently sought after, so you can expect the list to change from time to time.

4 Choose from the list of Trending topics presented, or, if your issue is not included here, scroll down to review the other categories offered

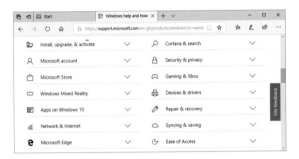

5 Select the category that covers the area of interest

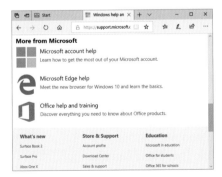

Right-click a topic or category and select Open in new tab or Open in new window, to keep the full list available for further investigations.

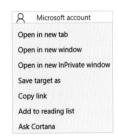

6 If your concern still isn't addressed, scroll down to investigate other sources of help and support offered

Get Help App

If you fail to find the answers you need with the usual help facilities, you can get help using the Get Help app.

You must be connected to the internet to use the Get Help app, and it is recommended that you are signed in with your Microsoft Account.

1 Select the entry for Get Help on the All Apps list

2 Get Help offers to assist you with problems in one of your Microsoft products

3 If the problem is related to ease of access, scroll down to contact the Disability Answer Desk, which provides specific support in that area

4 If you do have a product query, scroll back up to the initial screen

5 Enter a description of your problem and make sure to include the product you are using, then click the Next button to activate the search for related information

A plain language outline of your problem is best, since it will be matched against queries that other users have submitted.

...cont'd

6 Review the help content that is displayed to see if it directly addresses the issues that concern you

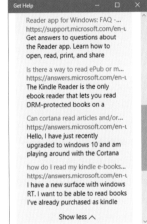

Select the heading of any entry to see the full text of the topic at the associated website.

7 Scroll down, and click Show more to reveal additional related items

8 If you don't find the answers you need, arrange a call from Technical Support to discuss your issue

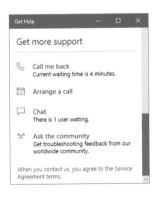

9 Alternatively, you can chat online with an Answer Tech, or connect with the Microsoft user community to review their questions and answers or suggestions

The Answer Tech will resolve basic issues for free, but you may be offered an upgrade to a fee-based service for more complex issues.

Windows Action Center

Messages and warnings from the Windows system and installed apps are displayed via the Notification area within the Action Center. To display the Action Center:

1 Swipe in from the right edge, or click the Action Center icon, which is now located to the right of Date/Time on the Taskbar

2 The Action Center opens as a full height bar, with alerts at the top and quick actions buttons at the bottom

The contents depend on the particular system. This image shows the entries displayed for a typical desktop PC. The Action Center for a Tablet PC will show Tablet mode turned on, and additional items such as Rotation lock.

3 You can click Collapse to reduce the number of buttons to four quick actions items

4 Click Expand to redisplay all the quick actions buttons

You can use Settings to change which quick actions buttons are displayed, and rearrange the sequence in which they appear in the Action Center.

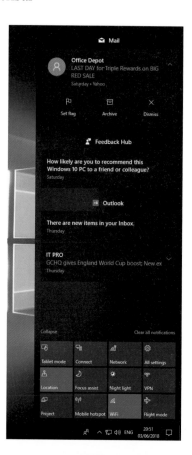

Hot tip

You can also open the Action Center by pressing WinKey + A.

Don't forget

If you are getting too many alerts, or want to avoid possible interruptions, right-click the icon and select Focus assist, then click Off, or choose Priority or Alarms only.

...cont'd

1 Select the All settings button, then System, then Notifications & actions, and then review and rearrange, or add and remove quick actions

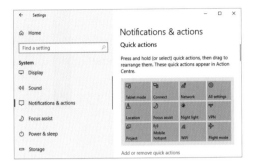

Hot tip

Again, these images are for a typical desktop PC, and the quick actions offered on other PCs may well differ.

2 Scroll down to select the types of notifications and manage different Notifications settings

Don't forget

You can choose to Hide notifications while presenting, to prevent pop-up notifications while you are using PowerPoint or projecting the display to a second screen.

3 Scroll down to select which apps will show notifications

Program Compatibility

If you're using applications designed to run under previous versions of Windows (prior to Windows 10), you may need to enable Compatibility mode to let them run correctly.

1 Type Compatibility in the Search box on the Taskbar, then select Run programs made for previous versions of Windows (the Program Compatibility Troubleshooter)

2 Click Next to find and fix problems with running older programs in Windows 10

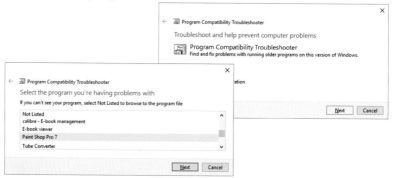

3 Select a program that may have problems, then click Try recommended settings

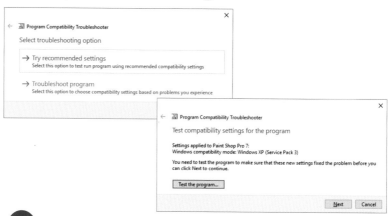

When it completes, select the appropriate result and take any actions suggested.

Troubleshooting has completed. Is the problem fixed?

→ Yes, save these settings for this program

→ No, try again using different settings

→ No, report the problem to Microsoft and check online for a solution

4 Click Test the program... to see if the selected settings were successful

Windows Defender

1 Click Settings, Update & Security, Windows Security, and then Open Windows Defender Security Center

Windows Defender provides protection against malicious software such as viruses and spyware, so you do not have to install separate utilities.

2 The Windows Defender Security Center opens to display the computer's latest status

Windows Defender also alerts you when spyware attempts to install or run, or when programs try to change important Windows settings.

3 Click Virus & threat protection to see details of the last check, and the status of protection updates

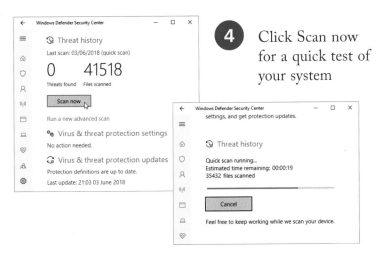

4 Click Scan now for a quick test of your system

Select Run a new advanced scan for a more comprehensive check of your system.

Windows Firewall

To protect your computer from malicious software while it is connected to the internet, you need Firewall software. This is included in Windows 10.

Entries may be added automatically when apps are installed; for example, when you download and install the Microsoft Solitaire Collection.

Windows Defender Virus and Firewall facilities will be turned off if you install a separate antivirus software product.

1 Open the Windows Defender Security Center (see page 229) and select Firewall & network protection

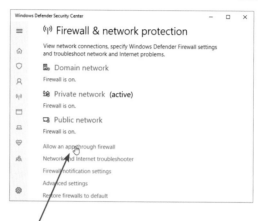

2 Click Allow an app through firewall, to view the list of allowed programs that can communicate through Windows Firewall

3 Click Change settings to make changes to the allowed apps and features, and to enable the option to allow another app to communicate in the same way

Allow another app...

Windows Update

To view the status of Windows Updates on your system:

1 Open Settings, select Update & Security and then click Windows Update

2 Check for updates if you wish, or View update history to see what updates have been applied

3 To let Windows Update know when best to apply updates, select Change active hours

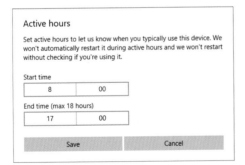

4 Select the Start or Finish time and scroll to select a new time

5 Click the Tick button to apply the new time, then click the Save button to confirm

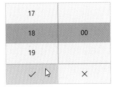

In Windows 10, Windows Update installs all updates automatically. At most you can defer updates for a time, but they will eventually be installed.

Windows Update may include some new apps, although updates to these and your other apps will be provided through the Store (see page 135).

Windows 10 updates are provided on a monthly basis, with significant updates such as the Creators Update and the April 2018 Update on a 6-monthly basis.

...cont'd

You can apply controls to the way Windows installs updates:

1 Open Settings, Update & Security and Windows Update then select Advanced options

If you are using a metered connection (where charges may apply) updates won't normally be downloaded.

232

- Get updates to other Microsoft products when you update Windows.
- Download updates even over metered connections.
- See notifications about restarting.
- Temporarily pause update installations for up to 35 days.
- Choose the branch readiness level, with one level for most people and another for organizational use.
- You can Defer Feature updates for up to 365 days.
- You can Defer Quality updates for up to 30 days.

Settings — □ ×

⌂ **Advanced options**

Update Options

Give me updates for other Microsoft products when I update Windows.
⬤ Off

Automatically download updates, even over metered data connections (charges may apply)
⬤ Off

We'll show a reminder when we're going to restart. If you want to see more notifications about restarting, turn this on.
⬤ Off

Pause Updates

Temporarily pause updates from being installed on this device for up to 35 days. When updates resume, this device will need to get the latest updates before it can be paused again.
⬤ Off

Pausing now will pause updates until 10/07/2018

Choose when updates are installed

Choose the branch readiness level to determine when feature updates are installed. 'Semi-Annual Channel (Targeted)' means that the update is ready for most people, and 'Semi-Annual Channel' means that it's ready for widespread use in organisations.

Semi-Annual Channel ⌄

A feature update includes new capabilities and improvements. It can be deferred for this many days:

365 ⌄

A quality update includes security improvements. It can be deferred for this many days:

30 ⌄

Deferring upgrades is designed to make business PCs more stable and allow systems administrators to test new feature updates before they reach their users.

Deferring Upgrades

Professional editions of Windows 10 allow you to choose to defer upgrades. If you enable this, you'll still receive security updates fairly swiftly, but you can put off downloading the feature updates for up to a year, making sure that they have been well proven in use.

Index

M

N

237